THE NAKED FACE

THE ESSENTIAL GUIDE TO
READING FACES

THE
NAKED FACE

THE ESSENTIAL GUIDE TO
READING FACES

Lailan Young

Illustrations by Rod Waters

St. Martin's Press
New York

Library of Congress Cataloging-in-Publication Data

Young, Lailan.
The naked face / Lailan Young.
p.   cm.
ISBN 0-312-11033-2 (pbk.)
1. Physiognomy.   I. Title.
BF851.Y67   1994
138—dc20   94-1575   CIP

First published in Great Britain by Random House.

First U.S. Edition: June 1994
10   9   8   7   6   5   4   3   2   1

To Mrs Blackbird

ACKNOWLEDGMENTS

I am grateful to many people, each of whom has a suitably propitious face: Doctor Helen Murphy, London medical practitioner, has the maintenance contract on my face and all its parts, except the eyes, which are carefully spied on by the ophthalmic surgeon, Patrick Trevor-Roper. The dentist, Naresh Bhuva, also added bite to the bits about teeth in the chapter on *Beauty and the Beast*.

Robin Young gave heartfelt support and expert textual criticism, and my dedicated and very kind agent, Dinah Wiener, worked hard to make my face fit. Lesley Sheringham, Monica Manwaring, Nina Miles, Celia Hornung Sanders, and especially Joy Berthoud all encouraged me to write this book.

Since I addressed the International Conference on the Meaning of Faces, which was organised by the British Psychological Society at the University of Wales in Cardiff, I owe much of my inspiration for this book from the fine work of some of the scholars who influenced the events at the conference, in particular Professors I. Eibl-Eibesfeldt, Sir E. Gombrich, Paul Ekman and Nico H. Frijda, Dr Jules B. Davidoff, and the writer-psychologist, John Liggett.

At Century the talented faces include Kate Parkin, the publisher who crystallised *The Naked Face*, my editor Cate Paterson, and publicist Cathy Schofield. The artist Rod Waters faced the challenge of bringing 169 facial features to life, while the designer Roger Walker gave the book its final face value.

The artists Prafulla Mohanti and Richard Lannoy spent hours giving advice during the writing and production of this book, and Lannoy was inspired by the book's title to paint his formidable version of *The Naked Face*.

Media man Michael Leapman, of *Barefaced Cheek* fame, tried to cure my computer illiteracy, but had more success in helping me to face up to the complexity of book production. His wife, Olga, helped me envisage the technique for providing an index.

And finally, my thanks go to American Airlines, British Airways and Virgin Airways for airlifting me to five continents for research. And I shall treasure for ever the faces and happy times spent with William and Ivy Gim, Pat Conway, Violet Lannoy, Elizabeth Salter, Juliette Lipeles, Lynn Fryer, Laurence Gilliam, Marcel Delannoy, Nazar Karagheusian, Egon Porhoroles, Pauline Hallam and Mrs Blackbird.

CONTENTS

THE NAKED FACE

THE ESSENTIAL GUIDE TO READING FACES

CHAPTER 1

THE NAKED FACE

The most distinctive, most recognisable and most memorable feature of any human being is the face. That is why the rich and famous have their portraits painted, and why many of us take snapshots of each other.

Like every personality, each face is individual and different. The idea that the face and the personality must in some way be related has fascinated people since the search for knowledge began, and it is still as compelling today.

Consciously or not we all make judgements about other people's faces. We say that someone has 'an honest face', 'a mean face' or puts on 'a brave face'. But frequently we reach those conclusions instinctively, on a hunch, and without either study or thought.

Not surprisingly, our first impressions, in which we place so much trust, often prove to be wrong.

The serious study of reading character from the face – the science of physiognomy – began, like so much else, in China. Even in the West, detailed attention to the science of interpreting people's character from their facial appearance dates back to the time of the classical scholars. Aristotle, Plato, Aristophanes, Hippocrates and Pliny all wrote at length on the subject.

In Imperial Rome, face reading was an honourable profession, but in England, Queen Elizabeth I decreed that anyone claiming to have knowledge of physiognomy or 'fantastical imaginations' should be 'stripped naked from the middle upwards and openly whipped until his body be bloody'.

The study was outlawed again in the reign of George II, yet despite such dire threats of punishment it continued to attract some of the country's greatest minds, including detailed research into face reading by the father of the theory of evolution, Charles Darwin, 130 years later.

My first book on face reading, *Secrets of the Face*, was devoted entirely to the Chinese masters' thoughts on the subject, which place great emphasis on the importance of facial structure and pay little regard to facial expressions or gestures.

After publication of the book I was invited to address the International Conference on the Meaning of Faces, organised by the British Psychological Society at the University of Wales. Delegates came from four continents, each a specialist in some aspect of the human face. I was inspired by the work which had been done in the field of facial expressions and gestures, by eminent psychologists, psychiatrists, anatomists and plastic surgeons around the world, and decided that I would write *The Naked Face* to bring together the latest and most important findings in a science which has intrigued people for so many centuries, and in which vital discoveries are still being made to this day.

There is a lot to see in any face. There are hundreds of different facial expressions and gestures, yet a competent interpreter of faces will be able to sift through the input of visible facial messages in a matter of moments, identifying those which provide the crucial clues to another person's feelings or likely course of behaviour.

Most people's inability to read the faces of others derives simply from the fact that they do not pay enough attention to them. We look at other people's faces, especially their mouths and eyes, more than we do at any other part of their body. Yet frequently we do not really 'see' what we are looking at, because we are too busy thinking about something else, or are not focusing our attention properly.

The face is the most compelling channel of communication, save speech, but just as we do not always hear or remember what others are saying, so we often fail to appreciate what their faces are signalling.

The best face readers are those who make a habit of looking into the eyes of other people, meeting their gaze and maintaining eye contact. Generally speaking, women are better at it than men. They are usually quicker at recognising faces, noticing when a person is unhappy, or ill, or pretending to be something that they are not. This is probably because women make eye contact with others more willingly than men would. In fact, women can usually sum up their subjects in about half the time a man would take.

But will their summing up be more accurate?

We all have a lot to learn by reading faces. There are a hundred or so muscles located just beneath the facial skin, distributed around fourteen bones. It is this amazing maze which controls the story book of the human face. If you can read it, each face will provide you with a story line to match a best-selling novel: there is love, hope and friendship, beauty, jealousy, deceit, treachery, spite, anger, greed, ambition, impatience, arrogance, smiles, laughter and tears, failure and success. And sex. All this can be read in the face of anyone you see or meet.

The Naked Face is the first book to bring together the international schools of face reading as they have evolved down the centuries since their conception in the ancient Chinese and Greek civilisations. I have taken account of advances in face reading research from many parts of the world, especially the United States, Canada, Japan, Germany, Switzerland, Belgium, France, Hong Kong and the United Kingdom.

In writing this book I have married the latest physiological and psychological research undertaken on the subject of facial analysis to the everyday needs of ordinary people, at work, at play, in friendship, sex, marriage, and long-term relationships, and in their family life. Of course one can apply a knowledge of face reading to the familiar faces of the important and famous, which are seen regularly in newspapers and on television screens. A knowledge of face reading will give you an inside look at the true personality and character behind their facial mask.

Yet far more important and beneficial in everyday life is learning how to read the faces of the people who matter to you today, tomorrow, and in the distant future. They may be your friends, workmates, bosses, advisers or rivals. The chances are that you will need to be able to anticipate their behaviour and personality to maintain and improve your relationships with them, to keep afloat and do well in the competitive times in which we live at the end of the twentieth century.

I hope *The Naked Face* will help you to better understand the minds and behaviour of your friends, spouse or lover, relatives and children, colleagues, neighbours and enemies – and all the strangers who will enter your life in the future. With face reading to guide you, they should be strangers no more.

CHAPTER 2

THE FIRST MINUTE

You are in the dentist's waiting room. He is running late and there are another two patients ahead of you, and both probably have toothache. Or you are waiting for a taxi, bus, train or aircraft and so are dozens of others, all impatient to be somewhere else.

Or, perhaps your friend, husband or colleague is late, and you are kept waiting in a hotel lobby, in a restaurant, or by the main entrance of a department store, theatre or cinema. Instead of looking at your watch every few minutes or showing the common symptoms of anxiety such as anger, impatience or frustration, you could be practising a spot of face reading for you have a ready supply of faces around you.

Many of us like to think we can make an assessment of others based solely on our first impressions; but many first impressions are off-target. Someone viewed at the outset as 'good' will acquire a 'halo' effect so that in subsequent meetings the face seems to reflect goodness and admirable qualities. The flattering halo is enhanced if the stranger has a pleasing appearance and if the first encounter takes place in an agreeable environment. But, likewise, once someone forms a negative impression of you it is much more difficult to get him or her to like you or ever to see your point of view.

Moreover, whether they be a president, premier, or neighbour, as long as we think they resemble ourselves we will over-estimate them. Many of us learn the hard way when someone we thought we could rely on lets us down: a lot of so-called friendships end or peter out like this.

There is another common reason for forming a faulty first impression: if someone reminds us of a person of whom we are deeply fond – for example, a loved grandparent – or makes us perhaps subconsciously recall someone we disliked, such as a feared maths teacher, we tend to transplant our feelings from one to the other.

People who are inclined to suppress their own display of emotion are extra-sensitive to the display of emotion in others. That introverts can better judge character and personality than extroverts will surprise many people, but in all likelihood extroverts are so busy experiencing the world and its peoples for themselves that they are unlikely to analyse and interpret the faces of those around them.

Other good interpreters of character and personality are individuals who are aesthetic, extremely sensitive, or intellectually sophisticated.

In the first minute a perceptive face watcher ought to be able to study a 'new' face and know if its owner is intelligent, impatient, trustworthy, mean or sensuous. Some of this information can be ascertained from the *structure* of the face. To verify your findings you will need to interpret *facial expressions* and *gestures*, which are described throughout the book.

Here, however, are a dozen suggestions for important characteristics which can be quickly discerned from reading readily visible features of the face, even when it is immobile or expressionless.

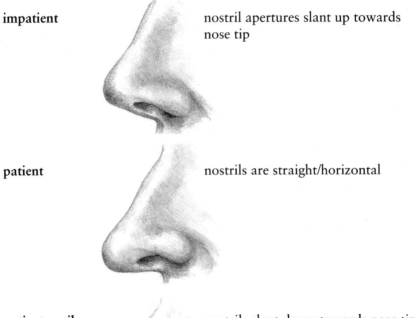

impatient nostril apertures slant up towards nose tip

patient nostrils are straight/horizontal

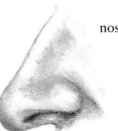

patient until riled, then 'explodes' nostrils slant down towards nose tip

jealous
- eyebrows join *or* copious growth of hair between eyebrows

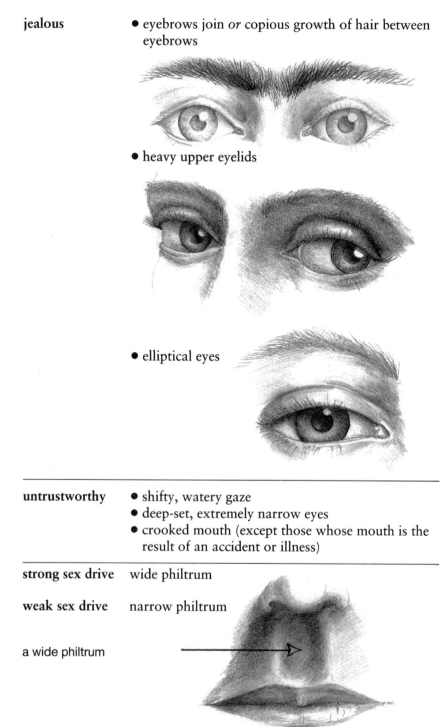

- heavy upper eyelids

- elliptical eyes

---

untrustworthy
- shifty, watery gaze
- deep-set, extremely narrow eyes
- crooked mouth (except those whose mouth is the result of an accident or illness)

---

strong sex drive   wide philtrum

weak sex drive   narrow philtrum

a wide philtrum

unfaithful	given the 'right' circumstances a lot of men and women would be unfaithful, but most likely are those whose upper lip is thicker than the bottom lip

sexual fulfilment is not easily found	small earlobes
very intelligent/ high IQ	a 'good' forehead: smoothly rounded, wide, high and deep, and free from blemishes
chilly/cold	• very thin lips • thin, angular nose • pointed chin and high, prominent cheekbones
friendly/ sociable	middle zone (eyebrows to nose tip) is longer than either the top or low zone

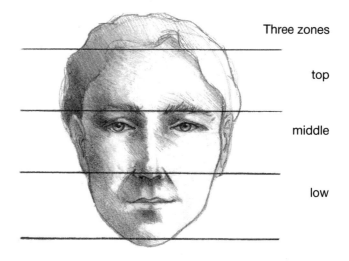

Three zones

top

middle

mean, generous the tighter and narrower the notch, the meaner is its owner in spirit and deed

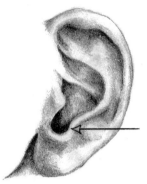

wide notch: generous

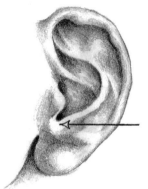

narrow notch: mean

How To Read Your Own Face and See Yourself as Others See You

We frequently find that we do not recognise ourselves in photographs, and many of us are disappointed, even dismayed, when we see ourselves on video film or television. 'Is that really me?' or 'Is my nose as big as that?' are common reactions. In fact, we probably prefer the faces we see in our mirrors to the real thing.

Of the three ways to read your own face, using a mirror is often the most convenient, but it does require honesty in noting the characteristics present in your face, and interpreting their significance according to the diagnoses in this book.

The second, and more thorough, way to read your own face is to have four photographs:

- *Full face*: smiling
- *Full face*: unsmiling, deadpan, neutral expression
- *Left profile*: deadpan, neutral
- *Right profile*: deadpan, neutral

To obtain a complete analysis it is important to keep your hair off your forehead, ears, and cheeks in the full-face images, and off the ears in the profiles. Otherwise, it will be difficult, perhaps impossible, to identify the type of hairline, temples and ear shapes you possess – all vital, telltale parts of the face.

A smiling full-face photograph allows you to interpret the smile, teeth and gums. An unsmiling portrait is necessary to reveal the general shape of the face, forehead, eyebrows, eyes and mouth, and in particular the angle and delineation of the line formed by the lips when the mouth is closed and relaxed. The two profiles permit a thorough examination of the formation of the ears, nose, chin and jaw.

A further route to self-knowledge is to have two photographs made to show up your 'two faces'. We are all two-faced in the sense that the left and right sides of our faces are asymmetrical, and never a perfect match. No face is exactly the same on both sides. Even the left side of the nosetip is different from the right side.

You will find it very revealing to create images of your two faces, the first as it would appear if the left-hand side of your face were mirrored exactly on the right-hand side; and the second as if the right-hand side were mirrored on the left. Technically these images are known as *chimerical facial composites*.

The way to make the images of your two faces is as follows:

- Have two prints made from a photographic negative of a full-face por-trait, one from the glossy side and the other from the dull. In that way you create a photographic image, and its reverse or mirror image.
- Cut the pictures in half down the centre.
- Combine the left side of one picture with the right side of the other, and vice versa.
- Copy and reprint the prints, retouching if you wish to remove the join.
- You then have two new faces of your subject, one made up of the right-hand side of the face married with its reverse image, and the other showing the left-hand side of the face coupled with its mirror image.

You will be amazed to see the two-faced you, and how different your two faces appear. But what can we learn from knowing how asymmetrical our faces are?

This question has concerned Chinese physiognomists since around 1800 BC, the Swiss and English for half a dozen generations, German scientists since the Thirties, and American, British, French and Belgian psychologists for the last fifty years.

Dr Martin Skinner, lecturer in psychology at the University of Warwick in England, and Dr Brian Mullen from Syracuse University, New York, analysed the findings of fourteen major studies of facial asymmetry, publishing the results in the *British Journal of Social Psychology* in 1991. One consistent finding in all the studies was that the left side of the face is more expressive than the right.

A suggested explanation for this phenomenon is that the left side of the face represents the private, personal and inner side of our personality. Influenced by the right hemisphere of the brain it reflects our basic emotions and attitudes. Some say that it shows up the *sinister* aspects of character – the word 'sinister' significantly being derived from the Latin for 'left'.

The right side of the face is the one we want to present to the world, the acceptable social mask behind which we attempt to conceal our real selves. It is like an advertisement hoarding on which we spread an ideal image for others to admire.

Influenced by the brain's left hemisphere, the right side of the face is the result more of our controlled responses, showing what we want others to believe of us.

The two faces of the great tenor, Luciano Pavarotti, make thrilling reading for the face watcher.

left-left   **right-right**

Pavarotti's two left sides
joined together.

His two right sides
joined together.

The Italian tenor's left side is much wider than the right, and it is the bucket-shaped face – wide across the forehead, tapering gradually to a strong, squarish jawline. The forehead of the left side is broad and smoothly curved while the right-sided forehead is considerably narrower and less rounded across the hairline.

His eyes in the left-sided portrait are narrower and more elliptical, but in the right side they are not only wider but note the area of white under the iris, which is absent from the other photograph.

The philtrum is the vertical channel which links the base of the nose to the middle section of the top lip. Note the different widths of Pavarotti's philtrum: in the right-right picture you can just see it as a narrow gap between the two sides of his moustache, while in the left-left portrait the philtrum is wider and more prominent. You can see more of his nostril apertures (slits) in the right-sided photograph, too.

His right-sided eyebrows are raised quizzically, but the inner corners of his eyes (closest to the nose) are more pointed in the left-left portrait. The significance of Pavarotti's facial parts is revealed in Chapter 13.

We are all familiar with the concept of conflicting emotions, and the ambivalence of human nature. In *Martin Chuzzlewit* Charles Dickens noted an example of conflict showing up in the face when he observed 'affection beaming in one eye, and calculation shining out of the other'. Such contradictions are easier to spot from the contrasting images created from the left and right sides of our faces.

You may, for example, find from the photographs of the two-faced you that you both smile and frown at the same time, one side of your mouth turning up while the other turns down. A picture made up of two left sides from anybody's face might scowl, while the same person represented in a picture composed of two right sides could be smiling.

The more symmetrical the facial expression the more honest, or the more wholly felt, any emotion displayed is likely to be. The more asymmetrical the more likely it is that the feeling is being forced or faked. A furious look that screws up one side of the face only is almost certainly put on. Equally a lopsided smile is likely to be insincere.

Just as short-term animation of the expression can reveal the state of our feelings at the moment, so habitual differences in the two sides of our facial expression can show up underlying contradictions in our personality. If, for example, the left corner of your mouth turns down while the right side turns up slightly, this asymmetrical appearance betrays a gloomy, morose nature behind a public display of cheerfulness.

We can adapt facial expressions to feign interest, sympathy or other emotions, but when emotion is genuinely felt it will show on our faces sooner or later, despite our best efforts to conceal it. For the attentive face reader, aware of the significance of facial asymmetry, the telltale signs are always present.

It requires conscious effort to discern these signs. Because it is directed by the brain's right hemisphere, it is our left eye which is most likely to be the one which perceives and registers more in quantity and in accuracy. As the left eye notices mostly what the right side face of a person opposite is telling it (because it is directly opposite their right eye), the chances are that we will overlook the person's deeper emotions and true feelings, which are more apparent on the left side of their face. If, for example, you want to know if a gift is *really* appreciated pay special attention to the expression on the left side of the recipient's face.

There is one further way in which the imbalance between left and right can provide useful information for face readers. Whenever people are asked a question which requires some thought before a response is given, they tend to look away before replying. Whether they look to their left or their right is not randomly determined, but is related to important aspects of personality and intelligence.

American research has shown that those who look away to the right are more likely to succeed at maths and sciences. That derives from the fact that the right hemisphere of the brain is usually predominant for spatial concepts and musical and analogical thought processes. Those who look away to the left are usually more suited to the classics or humanities, because the left hemisphere is dominant in verbal expression and reasoning.

CHAPTER 4

Basic Instincts

Good Humour

We smile when we are happy or amused. As an ardent student of face reading, Darwin identified some smiles as signals of tender feelings of love. P. G. Wodehouse enjoyed watching girls, seeing magic in their smiles which he likened to a raisin which, if it were dropped into the yeast of male complacency, would incite fermentation.

Although we smile in order to communicate with others, it is also an indication that at the time of smiling we do not wish to take any particular action. An example of this inactivity is the smile we use to signal an excuse or apology, for instance, 'I didn't mean to stand on your toe, but I was pushed by the person in front of me in the queue, so I'm sorry'.

Practically all of our facial features are involved in a smile, though what we are most conscious of are the muscles of mastication in play. While some smiles are broad and spread right across the face of the delighted person, others are mysterious and as enigmatic as the world's most famous smile, that of Mona Lisa (see Chapter 13).

The Japanese smile is often enigmatic, taking its cue from the days when Samurai women were required, like the women of Sparta, to express joy on hearing that their menfolk had perished in battle. To betray any sign of sorrow was a serious breach of their code of honour. Japanese greeting formalities occupy the whole face, head, and torso, which are tilted toward the other person, a display reminiscent of the old-fashioned shopkeeper's or salesperson's smile to signal 'I-aim-to-please'.

The frequent traveller, business executive or happy holiday-maker ought to know about the gamut of emotions that a smile conveys in other cultures. In Indonesia a smile may denote happiness or anger, while the Thais, Chinese, Koreans and Japanese will smile to express their confusion, embarrassment or even sadness. In many lands, smiling at a member of the opposite sex is taken as an invitation to flirt or have sex – in Sri Lanka, India, the Gulf States, and many nations of North Africa, for example.

In 1992 millions of workers and senior management in Eastern Europe were retrained by their business corporations in the ways of the West. Not only did this include courses in the use of the latest computers and machines but, in a much publicised series of courses organised in Potsdam, a former flight attendant for Pan-American World Airways, Gisela Tautz-Wiessner, instructed her students to smile while they were on the telephone. 'People can hear the difference,' they were told.

Not all smiles are warm. 'Smiling with cold teeth' is a Yiddish expression known in many homes around the world; or those fond of quoting Shakespeare might prefer, 'I can smile, and murder whiles I smile' from *Henry VI, Part 3*; or, 'There's daggers in men's smiles' in *Macbeth*. From *Hamlet* comes, 'One may smile, and smile, and be a villain'.

A smile is inaudible, but it can convey a clear message. A simple smile where the teeth are concealed signals smugness, mild pleasure, or that the person is smiling to himself, 'lost' in private thoughts.

The more usual smile, revealing the upper teeth, generally accompanies eye contact with another person, or a greeting such as 'How do you do?' or 'Glad to meet you'.

super-smile

Rarer by far is the smile in which only the lower row of teeth is displayed. This unusual smile is associated with the tentatively displayed signals of a lonely person, who feels inferior and unable to make social contact.

Both rows of teeth appear in a broad smile, when there is generally no eye contact, except at the end when the smile fades. A super-smile reveals both rows of teeth in addition to exposure of the gums, giving a 'gummy' expression of joy and pleasure.

Cold, insincere smiles are faked, looking every bit like the facial expressions of people patiently waiting for a photographer to focus and 'snap' the shutter. Or, a faked smile can be switched on, and switched off at lightning speed, lasting a fraction of a second and decaying before it reaches maturity. The difference between a lightning and a frozen smile is the duration. In addition, a frozen smile is less intense, but both lightning and frozen smiles are similarly false, faked and not genuinely intended.

A faked smile is accompanied by unsmiling eyes, and at times even a cold, hard stare. A heartfelt, genuine smile can last even after the other person or recipient of the smile has left the scene.

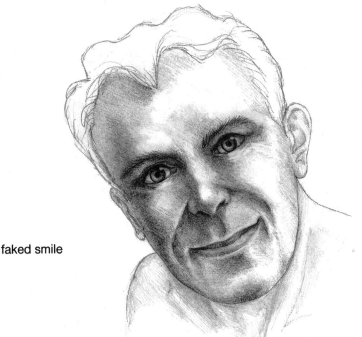

faked smile

Actors and actresses know that on-stage smiles need to be exaggerated, even if the recipient's face is only inches away, before the audience in the back row can see it. The skilful ones recognise that their faked smile must also include smiling eyes if they are to simulate the perfect stage smile.

As we get older we smile and laugh less. This is the result of maturing or ageing, and probably because, with friends around us smiling less, we fall in with the general pattern of social behaviour.

The great Charles Darwin, famous for his scientific theories but little known for the readings he made of his own children's faces, noted with great joy that his son started laughing at about fourteen weeks after his birth (psychologists today note an average of nine weeks).

Darwin reckoned the next best thing to happen to Homo sapiens after beginning to smile is the onset of laughter. Tickling usually does it, but

Darwin noted a young infant who screamed with fear if tickled by a stranger.

We have already recorded that psychologists think that when we smile we do not want to take any particular action at the time we smile. However, in laughter (and weeping), one's ability to act is impaired. We speak of people 'helpless' with laughter or 'prostrated' with grief.

Genuinely felt laughter was, to the American auctioneer and essayist Josh Billings, the sensation of feeling good all over, shown principally in one spot. Laughter, in fact, is a yelping, hooting or roaring sound, the mouth open and the corners elongated, the nose wrinkled, 'laughter' lines radiating out from the outer corners of the eyes, with the head often thrown back. If something is really worth laughing at, tears may even stream down the cheeks.

Sniggers involve exaggerated wrinkling of the nose and eye creases, distinguishable from a guffaw which includes a noticeable head throwback and little or no nose wrinkling.

As there is a faked smile so there is a forced laugh, when the eye muscles hardly or perhaps never move, making the eyes appear dull and expressionless. The Koreans and Chinese have words of warning about the involvement of our muscles in laughter, although their advice is inclined towards the stomach: 'Beware of someone whose stomach does not move when he laughs.'

Another giveaway of forced laughter is the man or woman who laughs too long or too loud, or both, at something that you might not think funny or amusing in any way. Perhaps they are not really amused, either, but try to hide the fact by laughing, or maybe they have not been listening to you but wish to convey their false appreciation by applauding you, as it were, by meaningless laughter.

Familiar to all of us are the occasions when we have missed a joke but are too embarrassed to admit it, so we laugh awkwardly, hoping our cover-up goes unnoticed. Most of us will have had to force a laugh at a party, in the office, or at a festive time such as New Year's Eve when someone asks a string of 'Do you know the one about . . . ?' On these occasions it is very easy to fall into the trap of 'laughing' at the bore's jokes too early, before he finishes his tale. An insensitive person will drone on, his eyes and ears closed to the bored faces and the sighs and yawns around him.

A person who laughs too frequently is either very, very happy or, more usually, embarrassed. Here, laughter is a way to reduce tension. Giggling can be a sign of secret sexual tension experienced by males and females, especially in Asian cultures, while many Africans express surprise, wonder and sometimes discomfort in the form of laughter.

However, we find Westerners are the people most likely to laugh if they see someone slip on a banana skin or when they are told that someone has died. They laugh to hide embarrassment and shock, but also to convey to others that they find it amusing that they are embarrassed. By closely observing the faces of your friends, acquaintances or total strangers as they smile or laugh you will learn to distinguish between expressions of genuine happiness and faked pleasure and well-being.

MONEY

Money is a favourite theme of writers, songwriters and philosophers. It can burn holes in your wallet or pocket, or in the words of novelist James Baldwin, money is rather like sex; you can think of nothing else when you are denied it, but once you have it you think of other things. A Cantonese saying adopts a more moral tone: 'It is harder to be poor without moaning than it is to be rich without being arrogant.'

Money-makers generally have big rather than small noses. The top of the ridge immediately below the bridge needs to be arched, the sides of the nose high, and the nostrils will not be visible when the nose is viewed from the front. A person's money-making potential is improved if the chin is strong, squarish or firmly rounded, and it helps if the chin actually protrudes. Furthermore, all of these qualities are enhanced if the ear lobes have a large, thick, fleshy and almost three-dimensional pad covering them.

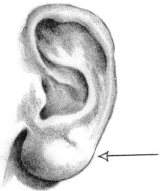

three-dimensional lobe

A receding chin should be taken as a strong warning not to play with investments, in particular on the stock exchange, nor should its owner make important financial decisions.

More warnings against taking risks with one's savings are issued to all those with short, bumpy or flat noses. Naturally you will wonder why. The answer is straightforward: you do not have a nose for business transactions or money matters, so you should heed the words of a Japanese sage who observed that 'As a dry finger cannot take up salt, so those with flat, short or bumpy noses find it hard to accumulate wealth.'

When we refer to someone as being mean, we usually think of money. However, the face watcher can tell at a glance those who are mean not only with money, but also mean in spirit. For example, you might have stopped a passerby in the street to ask the way, only to be told, 'I'm too busy (or in too much of a hurry) to stop and answer your question.'

The best and easiest way to judge whether a person is mean is to apply the notch test, described on page 88. Furthermore, if someone's gums show when they smile, this is a handy indicator that the owner of the gummy smile is inclined to be extremely generous to close friends and relatives and to anyone he or she particularly admires, otherwise this man or woman can be utterly mean.

A tight mouth, one which is pinched, mean and unforgiving in its clamped attitude, belongs to a person who is mean in every way: with money, time, charity donations, with his work colleagues, and to his or her unfortunate family.

tight, pinched mouth

Generosity can also be gauged from the notch test; the bigger the notch the more generous is its owner. The big problem about generosity is that being too generous arouses the suspicion that you could be trying to buy favours or praise. If you give someone a bottle of champagne he will heartily thank you; if you give two bottles he will think you got them free or at a bargain price, or that there is something wrong with them.

You can tell if someone is very generous to the point of being a spend-thrift: the inner corners of the eyes (closest to the nose) will be clearly pointed, like the tip of a newly sharpened pencil. It follows, of course, that such a man or woman is a bad money manager.

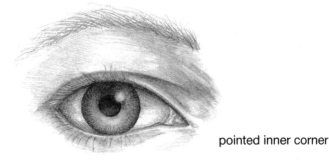

pointed inner corner

RELIABILITY

Throughout the pages of this book there are whole areas which will help you to judge whether or not someone you know is kind, a good friend, or reliable. These important aspects concerning a person's character will be found in particular in Chapters 7 and 9. There are seven additional features to complement these findings:

- When the mouth is closed and the lips at rest, a line forms where the lips meet: a wavy or rippling line is a sign of reliability.

wavy line where
the lips meet

- Pointed ear tips (top of ear) signal reliability.
- An acutely downward-pointing nose, resembling the nose of the Concorde, warns of unreliability, especially in friendship. It is also a sign of cruelty.

Concorde nose

- An unreliable person's eyes wander when he or she pretends to listen to you. They 'forget' commitments or promises. Their conversation consists of frequent usage of words like I, me, myself and mine. Lengthy monologues often replace conversation or an exchange of words. They will ask you a question, but will either answer it for you or ignore your reply by talking on and over whatever you might say.
- Gear-shifts are visible on the face of an unreliable man or woman as they think of something else more pressing, valid or beneficial to do after they have dumped, or rid themselves of, you.
- Anyone with a sleepy or drunken gaze or expression in their eyes will not prove a reliable friend or contact.
- Adroit at avoiding responsibility are those whose teeth are short, irregular, gappy and discoloured.

SELF-CONTROL, SPONTANEITY, FLEXIBILITY

Self-control is associated with straight eyebrows, which are much rarer than you would imagine, and with a long nose which has the additional distinction of a wide, straight ridge along its centre.

Lacking self-control are those without a *proper* ear lobe. This lack of ear lobe is a curiously common phenomenon, and if you look at, say, a hundred faces in the next day or so you might be surprised at the frequency of 'lobeless' ears.

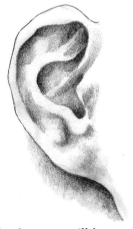

'lobeless' ear

To qualify as 'lobeless' an ear will have a stretch of flesh that filters straight from the rim or helix into the cheek. There is no bulbous 'end' or point at which the lobe, if it is present, hangs down.

Naturally, anyone who has a double or triple chin will lack self-control whenever food is available. The only exception to the excesses of good living and self-indulgence which multiple chins betray is the person with an ailment connected to weight gain or retention of fluids.

Inhibition is teamed with small mouths – more so if the lips are unusually thin. An extremely inhibited, withdrawn person will have lips so narrow that they are scarcely visible. Another indication of inhibition is a pair of nostril wings which the owner cannot flare; immobile nostril wings tell the world about their owner's limitations.

Spontaneity is allied to short eyebrows (a short eyebrow measures less than one and a quarter inches from the beginning by the nose bridge, to the tip) and to the flying forehead, which is an acutely sloping forehead from the hairline to the level of the eyebrows. Spontaneous men and women react quickly to events and to what others do and say to them, living for the moment and grasping every opportunity. As could be expected, they have difficulty concentrating on long-term goals, their thoughts and basic instincts alive to the endless challenges that life creates.

acutely sloping
forehead

Independent and non-conformist are those whose ears are big, wide, thick and protruding. While many of us have one or two of these features, few of us possess the clutch of all four, necessary to qualify as independent-minded non-conformists of high calibre.

In all probability the only person in the world who knows if you are flexible or intractable in your ways, thoughts and outlook is your dentist. For it is the tip of the tongue which provides the answer. A slim, light tongue tip belongs to those able to adjust to the prevailing or changing circumstances. They can change or modify their ways and outlook as situations alter. On the other hand, there are many who simply cannot amend their ways. They are left flat-footed, unable to move with the times. Their tongue-tips will be heavy and obtrusive.

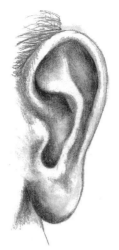

big, wide, thick,
protruding ear

slim, light
tongue tip

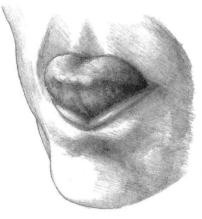

heavy, obtrusive
tongue tip

PESSIMISTS AND OPTIMISTS

A case of 'doughnut psychology' was finely observed by the writer McLandburgh Wilson, who noted that an optimistic person can see the doughnut while a pessimist can only see the hole.

Pessimists are disgusted with just about everyone and everything but themselves. They 'tut-tut' about young people's loud music, they disapprove of computers, long-haired males and topless girls at the beach. 'What is the world coming to?' is their fearful cry.

Optimists want to experience new things, trying out anything innovatory or unfamiliar. They often carry organ donor cards.

A quick look at the corners of the eyes and of the mouth will pinpoint the optimist and the pessimist. In all probability the corners will drop or slant down on the pessimist's face, and they will slant up if they belong to an optimist. It is worth noting, too, that the corners of the mouth droop even on the faces of unhappy children.

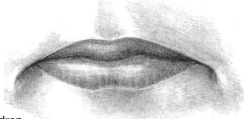

mouth corners drop

An optimist's eyelashes turn up naturally and without the help of eyelash-curlers. A super-optimist, one who *always* looks on the bright side of even the most horrible situations, is often distinguished by a totally smooth forehead; the forehead could be narrow or broad, but it will be quite free from bumps, blemishes, ridges or any type of protuberance.

A super-pessimist will almost always have deep lines emanating from the corners of the mouth, descending in a circular pattern towards and around the chin. If the lines are especially deep they reveal disquieting disgust, suspicion and a total lack of confidence in anyone or anything.

ON BALANCE

To be intelligent, adaptable and energetic in about the same proportions is one definition of a well-balanced person. If they have it in them, their faces will tell us all about their laudable balancing act.

three zones

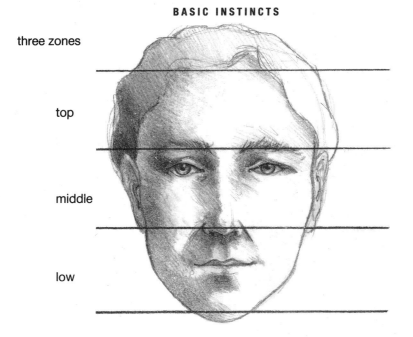

top

middle

low

Firstly, the three zones of the face will be equal in width: top zone, from the hairline to the eyebrows; middle zone, from eyebrows to nose tip; and, low zone, from nose tip to chin.

Next, a nicely rounded, protruding chin adds to the owner's stability and well-being, and is a sign of sociability, too. Nor is there any disadvantage if your chin and jaw are slightly squarish or straight, for this denotes enormous determination to get things done with a minimum of fuss: this would include anything from cleaning the house to buying a car.

Human beings have a nasty habit of labelling as unstable anyone who behaves 'differently'. A face watcher will be able to fit a certain type of eyebrow to this individual: someone who is at odds with family, friends and colleagues will very likely have eyebrow hairs growing down. Only

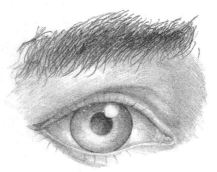

hairs grow down

the very perceptive will ever have noticed that most eyebrow hairs grow or lie sideways; much rarer are eyebrow hairs growing downwards. Historians, serious face watchers and the French alike might be interested in the fact that General Charles de Gaulle had a fine pair of eyebrows with hairs growing down in the direction of his cheeks and his army boots.

Immature and unpredictable in what they might say or do are those with:

- pouting lips (also a giveaway for those who sulk)

- a dimple in the chin (midway between the lower lip and jaw line)

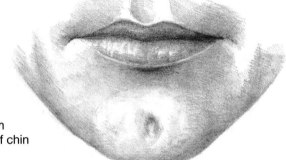

dimple in
centre of chin

- a babyish forehead: domed, bulbous, too big for the rest of the face

babyish forehead

BABIES, CHILDREN, INVALIDS AND SENIOR CITIZENS

Babies, young children, invalids and senior citizens have something in common. At some time or another they need to be cared for. How then can you choose from the host of applicants or 'possibles' who should mind your old grandmother, babysit your children, take your invalid brother to the hospital, or collect your son or daughter after school, while you work?

The best advice from a face-reading point of view is to look for some of the finer qualities described in this chapter, among them reliability, happiness, sense of humour, optimism, intelligence and energy.

Chapter 7 includes ways to identify friendliness, warmth, generosity, sincerity, kindness and compassion, all of which are desirable qualities that a babysitter, childminder and granny watcher should possess.

CHAPTER 5

THINK TANK

How do we recognise who is intelligent? We talk about people, or animals for that matter, having an intelligent expression – which probably means they look alert, have bright eyes, or seem to understand what is going on. Most of us readily credit others with intelligence if they agree with what we say.

The normal way to measure intelligence is by a formal and complicated battery of IQ tests. Yet it is possible to gauge people's intelligence from their faces.

The forehead is the key to the face watcher's guide to spotting the brainy ones among friends, relatives and colleagues. A 'good forehead' is one which is wide, deep and smoothly rounded. If these qualities are present their owner will learn fast, acquiring knowledge with little effort.

An especially wide forehead, which is also deep, smoothly curved and free of blemishes and bumps, denotes an active, quick intellect. However, the bearer of this forehead confines his or her interest in energetic physical exertion to sexual activities. This man or woman would probably be considered a 'stick in the mud' by colleagues and certainly by neighbours and casual acquaintances.

The three zones of the ear provide the face reader with more data. The top zone represents the intellect. The middle zone shows a person's ability to communicate. The low zone reveals whether or not a person is physically inclined; attracted, for instance, by exercise and keeping fit, food and drink, travel or anything that could be described as 'good living'.

Whichever zone is the largest (taking into account the width and length of each zone) is considered the dominating aspect of its owner's mind and interests.

A very large top zone pinpoints a gift for logic and abstract thinking. You will also find that those who tend to think in abstract terms make more eye contact with you than those who think in more concrete terms.

three zones of the ear

top

middle

low

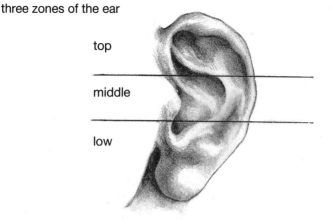

This is because abstract thinkers are less likely to be put off by being watched by another person.

Many of us find an intellectual with his feet on the ground a very agreeable companion. Not only will he or she entertain us with facts and information about the lives of great artists or how electricity works, but they will also be able to mend fuses or help paint the ceiling. Evidence of practical skills is a very thick, fleshy, smooth helix (the outer rim of the ear).

Most of us would be far too embarrassed to stare at anyone with a squint, largely because we can never be sure whether or not they are look-ing at us. However, if you are prepared to have a go at reading a squint, note that a right eye which is directed upwards and out signals above-average intelligence, whereas a similarly directed squint in the left eye (up and out) is a sign of irrationality.

According to the Italian criminologist, Cesare Lombroso, born criminals have very large, thick, rounded ears, too large in fact to match the proportions of other parts of their face. Lombroso attributed great in-telligence to congenital criminals, but he noticed a diminution of their mental powers if the lobes were thin and attached to the side of the head instead of hanging freely (see page 194).

Attached or affixed ear lobes are associated with men and women who know their weaknesses, and are prepared to take measures to overcome or nullify them. This ability to admit to a fault is especially valuable in a leader or trend-setter. For instance, presidents, prime ministers or com-pany directors who are aware of their weakness in a particular aspect of policy-making will appoint to their cabinets or boards competent speci-alists in these sensitive areas.

As the face can signal the very bright individuals so too can it reveal the less gifted, small-minded individuals. In many nations women are thought to lack intelligence. In Russia and Romania there is a popular saying that women have long hair and short brains, while the dismissive proverb in Bosnia and Serbia is: 'A woman cuts her wisdom teeth when she is dead.'

It takes a brave man or woman to look at their face in a mirror to search for the characteristics of low or restricted intelligence. Here are a few tell-tale signs:

• ears that do not reach eye-level	limited intelligence; low self-esteem
• bumpy, very narrow, pointed forehead (at the top)	unable to keep up with others in a discussion; dithers
• concave band across mid-forehead	bad memory
• flat or concave band under eyebrow hairs	slow to catch on
• indented area between eyebrows	lazy, because they do not make good use of mental powers
• joined eyebrows	lazy; do not use their mental gifts; uneven concentration
• hairy mid-forehead	feel intellectually inferior; poor concentration
• hair covers temples or pulse points on side of forehead	diminished reason and logic (see page 73)
• forehead slopes forward and bulges very noticeably over the eyes	mental instability

forehead bulges
over the eyes

38

Most of us will never win a Nobel, or any other prize for brain power, though a lot of us do well with plenty of common sense, getting more out of life than many of the most gifted men and women of our time. The facial signs of abundant common sense include:

- a prominent or raised band across the lower forehead, over which the eyebrows grow;

- eyebrow tips slant towards centre of ear; and

- a square-shaped, or squarish, ear

squarish ear

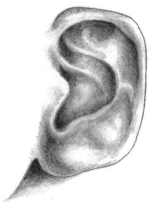

A BIRD'S EYE VIEW

A cruising bird of prey can see its dinner scurrying along a river bank in a deep valley below its flight path. Some people have a similar uncanny knack of fastening on to things others might easily overlook.

You think you look good today, wearing a nice social face, hair newly trimmed, a friendly smile, until a friend says with unnerving accuracy: 'You're not happy, are you?' Both bird of prey and the friend are perceptive, or as the common adage has it: 'Some people have eyes in the back of their heads'.

As you might expect, the more perceptive among us are distinguished by having widely spaced eyes. Like a bird's they are better for seeing around with a bold, broad sweep.

Perceptive people are likely to suffer more because they foresee and anticipate events and actions before most of us catch on to the fact that anything important is happening.

There are a number of facial traits to look for in your search for intuitive and perspicacious men and women:

- eyes set wide apart;
- fine eyebrow hairs;
- narrow eyebrows;
- a bump or elevated ridge under the eyebrows;
- narrow eyes;
- a fleshy, undulating mouth (fleshy lips joined by a wavy line visible when the mouth is shut and relaxed);
- a protruding mouth; and
- wide, fairly round, generous nostrils.

You can assess how perceptive or intuitive you are by participating in a perception test. If you can give six or more reasons why people momentarily bite their bottom lip you are quite perceptive. Here is a selection:

- shy, embarrassed;
- sudden physical effort;
- while suppressing pain;
- while feeling pain, such as sitting on a pin;
- if they are about to lie or say or do something dishonest;
- when remembering something they have forgotten to do;
- while intently listening to something personal;
- while concentrating;
- with sudden tension or anxiety;
- if they are one of the 'big boys' or 'men of true grit' who do not cry, but bite their lips and clench their hands instead;
- to express sympathy, dismay, or concern when someone is telling bad, disconcerting, unusual, or exciting news; and
- to express admiration.

If you had any more ideas, then you probably have all or most of the facial features that go with perception. Moreover, you will have a considerable understanding of yourself and of others, too.

MEMORY

If our memory is good we are compared to an elephant; if it is bad, to a sieve. Rudyard Kipling referred to a man's feat of memory when he wrote that 'Some women'll stay in a man's memory if they once walked down a street'. But for Samuel Johnson a man's age had also to be considered: 'If a young or middle-aged man, when leaving company, does not recollect where he laid his hat, it is nothing; but if the same inattention is discovered in an old man, people will shrug up their shoulders, and say, "His memory is going."'

Face reading experts identify a good or a bad memory from the forehead, eyes and ears as the following chart shows.

Good memory

Who?	Which facial feature/gesture?	Memory for
Chinese school	very smooth mid-forehead (the band midway between eyebrows and hairline)	facts, figures
French school	rectangular-shaped forehead (straight sides, wide, quite deep)	most things
Greek and Vietnamese schools	long lobes	general knowledge; literary quotes
Austrian school	eyes set wide apart	verbal/conversational exchanges
Belgian school	round, large, protuberant eyes	things learnt by rote (by repetition without regard to the meaning)

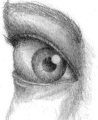

round, large, protuberant eyes

Bad memory

Chinese school	indented, bumpy, hollow in mid-forehead	generally forgetful, often maddeningly so
Belgian school	very deep-set or sunken eyes	events; confidential information
Almost universal	slap our forehead with the palm of the hand when we forget something	

CONTEMPLATION AND CONCENTRATION

When we are thinking about something, or trying to remember a 'forgotten' fact or instruction, our face may appear glum, the corners of the mouth drooping somewhat, eyes 'far away' or focused on an unseen object so that another person might be unintentionally misled into thinking we are gazing at an important object, person, scene or event somewhere behind them or to one side.

Contemplation can, therefore, look like boredom or inattention, and sometimes depression. So, in order to know who are the pensive, reflective among us it is safer to look at the general shape of the face.

round nose tip;
plump nostril wings

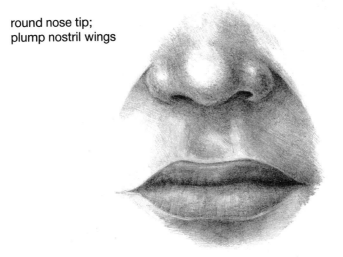

A round nose tip and plump nostril wings are a strong indication of a person's deep understanding of how others feel, especially in times of crises. Tough on themselves because they set high standards of personal behaviour, most men and women with this type of nose subscribe to what used to be known as the 'old school' of good manners, where law and order were observed to the letter, where respect was shown to old people (such as giving up one's seat to an elderly person in a bus or train), and where promises made meant promises kept.

Reflective and cogitative, too, are those whose faces are squarish in shape, that is, as wide as they are deep or long. Winston Churchill had a square face, and he portrayed most of the features closely associated with this type of face; a square-faced man or woman knows when to act or when to hold back, when to be pushy or patient. When the mind of a square-faced person is made up he or she will see the project through to the bitter (or sweet) end.

square face

Long eyebrows that stretch from the bridge of the nose right down the sides of the forehead (below the pulse points) generally denote a degree of lateral thinking or the ability to think through problems for possible solutions. And so, too, does a mole in the 'E' position.

If you look at the mole chart on page 155, mole E is situated anywhere between the end of the eyebrows and the hairline on either side of the face. Owners of this mole are pensive, but also melancholic at times. And for apparently inexplicable reasons they are envied for their achievements (which might be minor) and lifestyle (which could be quite ordinary).

On a different note, it could be valuable to know that when someone is blinking slowly it is usually because he or she is thinking something through, weighing up a situation. If you are hoping for a favour or a good judgement from this person you would be well advised not to interrupt his thoughts.

Facial signs of concentrated attention vary from culture to culture. Researchers in America and the British psychologist and prolific author on the subject of eye contact, Michael Cook, have shown that people look at each other only half as often while talking (and thinking) about a difficult topic as when chatting about a trivial or less important matter. On the other hand it has also been noted that Arabs stare at each other more directly and intensely if they are engaged in an especially urgent exchange of ideas. And if you have ever discussed important issues, such as, say, business practices, with a Chinese, you will probably have been uneasily aware of his or her hard, penetrating stare.

If you are from a Western nation you are likely to have been embarrassed and baffled by the apparent rudeness of the way the Chinese stare directly at you. Many people stare if they intend to give you their undivided attention. By concentrating their mind whole-heartedly on the matter, they feel able to make a better judgement or assessment of the situation.

When we have to think hard about a matter that requires a quick decision, it is very likely that our corrugator muscles (located at the inner extremity of the eyebrows) gather or bunch up into a 'furrowed brow' on a level with the eyebrows. This is also likely to occur if we are worried or burdened, but then the brow is likely to remain more constantly furrowed over a longer period of time.

furrowed brow

It is more difficult to see from the face's structure who will have good powers of concentration, but those with the greatest chance of possessing this useful quality are those with deep-set eyes. Conversely, those with wide-open eyes cannot evaluate what they take in before the next influx of information, simply because they see too much through their big, wide-open eyes.

Anyone whose eyebrows grow fairly close to the eyes is admirably suited to any work which requires reflection, evaluation, and making decisions which affect many people. However, if the eyebrows are so close to the eyes that they could be described as 'pressing on the upper eyelids' you can take this as a sure sign of impatience. As might be expected, eyebrows that are far away from the eyes will act as a barrier preventing concentration; such eyebrows, moreover, signal a predilection to waste energy by striving to attain goals that are out of reach and beyond the competence of their owner.

eyebrow
close to eye

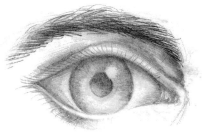

There are seven more facial features which disclose bad or limited powers of concentration:

- very steeply arched eyebrows;
- very pointed inner corner of each eye (corner nearest the nose bridge);
- upper lip which is noticeably shorter than the lower lip (that is, shorter from one corner of the mouth to the other);
- chaotic eyebrows (untidy growth, different hair lengths, bare patches, or an erratic shape);

chaotic
eyebrow

- curly eyebrows, which also tell of unsystematic minds and fickleness;

curly
eyebrow

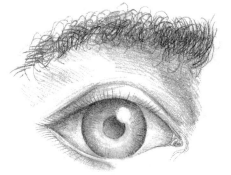

- a sleepy gaze (permanent), which also reveals faint-heartedness and, if the person is employed, a need for supervision to make sure he gets down to work; and
- a bump or swelling right in the centre top of the forehead, immediately by the hairline. This person also *appears* to be timid and slow to react, but beware of possible deception for this could be a clever attempt at a cover-up to buy time before making a decision.

Good powers of concentration are required to grasp and take maximum advantage of what is going on in the present; another intellectual gift is required if we are to plan for the future. Many of us save money for a 'rainy day', uncertain of what the future might hold. In the event, it often proves we have put our trust in inappropriate investments, which fail to meet our eventual needs.

For clues as to who the fortunate men and women with the gift of foresight will be, look for Tiger eyes which, according to oriental face watchers, are rectangular in shape, all-seeing in their sweep across the horizon and, as it were, beyond into the unknown (see page 57).

However, some people cannot, as the popular saying acknowledges, see beyond the end of their noses. Many who lack foresight are remarkable for having eyebrows which are much paler than their head of hair; their eyebrows are usually scant, too.

SPIRITUALITY

Millions of people on every continent fail to understand why tens of thousands of Britons, Indians, Pakistanis, Australians, New Zealanders, Sri Lankans, South Africans, West Indians and Pacific Islanders want to play the game of cricket. The British peer, Lord Mancroft, explained the origins of cricket as the invention of the non-spiritual English in order to bestow upon themselves a feeling and a concept of eternity.

There are certain ways and means to identify the spiritual among us, for whom the soul, spirit and creative thought are as real and vital as the body. They would be happier discussing questions about the meaning of life, or whether there is an after-life in which we might meet our loved ones again, than participating in an exchange of gossip or tales from the boardroom or shop floor.

Estimates from America suggest that about two-thirds of adult Americans believe in hell, while only about a quarter of the British do. Spirituality is a strong force in black cultures, too, where it emphasises the vital enjoyments and experiences that can be found in life independent of mechanical influences and material well-being.

A man or woman whom we might consider as being spiritual can hold another's gaze with peace and without a trace of nervousness, challenge or defiance. The gaze could be described as worldly, wise and calm. These same eyes will scan another's face with interest and concern.

In addition, the mouth might sympathetically mimic another's lip movements, expression, or anticipate the words before they are expressed. For instance, a very sensitive person will do this while he or she is listening to an account of a person's witnessing a horrible road accident, by conveying through eye movements and lip movements genuine feelings of 'I'm so sorry for you' or 'I understand how shocked you are to have been there when it happened.' In other words, those of us gifted with spiritual qualities and 'insight' into the thoughts and minds of others can be a great comfort and source of strength in time of need.

I have noted that many spiritual people have a hint of a smile lurking permanently around their lips, or eyes, or sometimes both. This is not the look of a fool or simpleton; on the contrary, it indicates intelligence and insight.

More inclined to be superstitious than spiritual are those men or women with round faces and round (or rounded) hairlines. If you are very observant you will also be able to point the finger at those who are both superstitious and spiritually disturbed. This challenge to a face reader's skill needs careful diagnosis.

In Chapter 9, you will see that an eye with three whites (white areas on each side of the iris, plus another either above or below the iris) shows its owner to be extremely sensitive. Add to this a dull, lacklustre gaze and you will have before you someone who is spiritually troubled by self-doubts and a fear of losing his or her way in what will always be a troubled existence. For some, suicide will be a recurring thought.

Many thought-provoking writers and philosophers are distinguished by having this unusual combination of features of the eyes.

CREATIVITY

Every morning Marcel Proust turned a spoon in his coffee cup, each time seeing there a new view that was different from yesterday's and tomorrow's. His creative mind permitted a perpetual renewal even in so small and ordinary an object.

You do not have to spend all your time watching how they stir their coffee to know if someone is artistic. The most supremely creative of all will have a beautiful mouth, one with a 'point of refinement' and a 'point of sensibility'.

The point of refinement is the tiny dip at the centre of the upper lip, as shown on page 96. If a vertical line joins this point to the bottom of the upper lip in a rosebud-shaped mouth, the owner of this artistic mouth will be delicately creative in love-making too.

The point of sensitivity is a downward point or minute arrowhead which fits into the lower lip like a tiny jigsaw piece (see page 97). Those lucky to have both creative points are destined for stardom. Whether or not they reach for the stars and make it to the top will depend on one vital decision: identifying the art form or career at which they excel, ignoring the appeal of another which might pay more in financial rewards, but which will be more successfully done by another star for which it was intended.

For example, many highly talented musicians decide to form their own group or band instead of going solo, never quite realising their star potential. Others think they have the star qualities of an Elvis Presley or a Madonna and try for recognition as solo performers, but most never reach the starry heights of their idols. Or, many artists look for a job in a publishing house and spend their lives designing book jackets or garish magazine covers when they might have persevered with their easel and brushes by a river bank.

The true 'ideas' man or woman with the best concepts and the most original, creative and fertile mind also has a correspondingly 'artistic' forehead – wide, deep, smoothly rounded and largely free from bumps, dips and ridges. However, if a fine forehead is accompanied by a thin, narrow or pointed chin, this combination of artistic traits reveals to the face watcher that the artistic person is better thinking up ideas than putting them into effect. In other words, it is no use hoping to go far in the arts and creative work unless you are able to stay with the project to which you are committed, finishing it with the same flair and enthusiasm with which you began it.

There is an exception. If a person can come up with new ideas and thoughts as easily as you or I can breathe, he or she ought to be given the freedom to create, leaving the follow-up work to be done by a back-up team.

Those with an artistic forehead, as described above, who also have a top zone (of the forehead) that widens noticeably along the hairline, will have a potent way with words. As this type of hairline denotes imagination, logic and love of philosophy, the prospective writer could quite easily turn his or her mind to fiction or non-fiction, possibly producing both with flair and ease.

We express taste and artistry in the way we dress, furnish and decorate our homes, the type of food and drink we like, and what we do for leisure, recreation, and vacations. Difficult though it may be to admit, it has to be

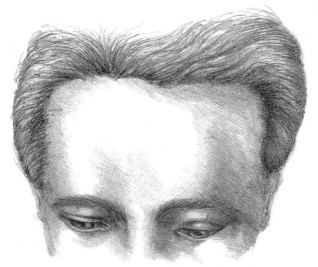

top zone of forehead widens along hairline

said that we all have some artistic qualities, however obscure or idiosyncratic they might look to others.

Writing in *Metropolitan Life* in 1978 Fran Lebowitz argued that very
few individuals are capable of true artistic ability, and with her customary
wit urged anyone with a burning desire to write or paint to cast aside the
longing by eating something sweet. That way, she suggested, the creative
urge would go away.

The following chart provides an at-a-glance guide to identifying artistic, creative people. It also includes clues to the *poseurs*, who affect to
know and understand the ways of art and artists.

Face Part	Distinguishing feature	Type of artistry or creativity
outer rim of ear (helix)	paler than rest of ear, or bumpy	serious ideas; 'I have a theory about that . . .'
hairline	M-shaped, with either pointed or rounded edges	sensitive to line, form, colour; enjoys being in the limelight; seeks fame
eyebrows	arched	generally imaginative; clever with words in conversation with friends or close associates; bad concentration; kind; creates ways to please those whom he or she likes or admires

Face Part	Distinguishing feature	Type of artistry or creativity
eyebrows	one higher than the other	fertile imagination; can produce a fast flow of ideas and suggestions; generally has feet on the ground, but occasionally lapses into unworkable, impracticable schemes
eyebrows	raises them while at the same time 'talks' with the hands	the act of using the corrugator muscles and raising the eyebrows, combined with expressive movements of the hands is sometimes described as the 'mad professor' look, associated with the learned, enquiring, inquisitive minds of scholars, inventors, creators
eyebrows and forehead	plentiful growth of hair between the eyebrows and a heavy band of horizontal wrinkles on the low zone (above the eyebrows) of the forehead	this man or woman is narrow-minded; unimaginative; jealous

hair between eyebrows; heavy band of wrinkles

Face Part	Distinguishing feature	Type of artistry or creativity
cheeks	well-defined lines (furrows) radiating out from the nostril wings to curve down the lower cheeks and around the mouth corners	resourceful; takes the initiative; ideas galore
nose	a round nose tip	artistic especially in dress, home design and décor; possible writing ability; daring colour sense; a round nose tip is a sign of honesty
mouth	an upward curving line where the lips meet when the mouth is closed and in repose	improvisatory; could create unusual jazz, board games, or clothes; persuasive *and* scheming
mouth	an overhanging top lip (see page 113)	very imaginative; has a strong sex drive
mouth	teeth protrude	a dilettante attracted to 'the arts' superficially; the type who enrolls for a study course in creative writing, music, painting, cookery, or wine-tasting but rarely completes it
nose	long, narrow	a dilettante in the fine arts; often witty and engaging

CHAPTER 6

ON THE JOB

Active adults are expected to spend about a quarter of their lives at work. The British philosopher, Bertrand Russell, distinguished two kinds of work: doing it, and telling other people to do it. He found that the former was unpleasant and ill-paid, while the latter was pleasant and highly paid.

Whether we are a boss and supervisor or a labourer or somewhere in between, work is a central and intrinsic part of our life. We go to work to provide essentials such as food and shelter, and to purchase luxuries like holidays. Directly or indirectly work provides most of the things that bring joy or challenges to our lives.

We might work to achieve promotion, or with the object of starting our own business, but, like it or not, most of us put effort into our jobs through fear of punishment in one form or another. Even at the very top, chairmen and directors must work to impress, and keep the favour of, their company shareholders. Top executives are answerable to the board.

Middle management has to prove itself fit for promotion, and deliver results to retain employment. Employees at the bottom of the heap can be penalised for a whole gamut of misdemeanours, ranging from bad time-keeping to taking too many private telephone calls or being rude to customers.

Wherever people are employed there is a set of rules and conventions that employees are expected to observe. Employees have to adapt to the requirements of their job and their position in the workforce if they are to keep their job or ever be promoted.

Most employees work together better as a team if they share similar ideas about achieving the best results and if they like each other and are on friendly terms. The face reveals a lot about a person's ability to be a good, reliable friend, and there is more about making friends in Chapter 7.

While friendship at work is a good thing, a person needs far more qualities to succeed in a career. Whether you are new on the job market and still struggling to find a footing, or well on the way to the top, or even already at the top and thinking about whom to select for a newly vacant position in your company or office, being able to recognise from a person's face strengths and weaknesses of character and personality is one more valuable weapon at your disposal as you ponder the future of your own career or that of the people who depend on your judgement.

Some people prefer to work at their own speed and in their own way, without a boss or direct supervisor watching them. They dislike accountability, preferring to be judged by results rather than by their methods of achieving them. Anyone with a steeply angled middle to their eyebrow is likely to prefer being their own boss, and will be best suited to following some kind of self-employment, perhaps as a taxi driver, writer, freelance photographer or musician.

steeply angled
middle eyebrow

The majority of us, however, need or prefer to be on someone else's payroll, planning a lifestyle based on the regular arrival of the pay packet or monthly salary cheque.

THE INTERVIEW

At the start of a career, and whenever applying for promotion, employees have to face an interview for the job they have set their sights on. Before going to the interview the applicant should, of course, have seriously considered how appropriate he or she will be for the type of work that is involved. In doing that a good hard look at one's own face can reveal vital information about one's strengths and weaknesses and where one's aptitude lies.

Equally, though, the interviewers will be closely observing the interviewees' faces for telltale signs of who will best meet their requirements. There are already employers who make their choice of candidates on the basis of analysing their facial characteristics. This method of personnel selection is used in countries where the art of face reading is most highly developed, particularly in Hong Kong and Taiwan, but it is gaining popularity in Western Europe, notably France, in the United States, South America, Australia and New Zealand.

What follows will, therefore, be of interest both to young hopefuls applying for their first job, and to seasoned professionals with the responsibility of hiring or promoting employees. Both should make full use of what the face, through its structure, expressions and gestures, can tell them about personal characteristics as they affect employment prospects and job suitability.

There are a number of facial do's and don'ts which are strongly advocated for those who are anxious to make a good impression at an interview.

DO: Turn your face fully towards those conducting the interview, even if you have to move your chair to be in this position. Looking sideways will make you feel ill at ease. Remember that sidelong glances may give the impression of slyness or diffidence. 'This candidate did not look us in the eyes' is a possible comment from a prospective employer, and one to be avoided.

DO: Show that you are listening to what the interviewers say. Be attentive. You can make this evident by establishing frequent eye contact with each member of the panel either as they address you, or by looking at each in turn.

DO: Show that you are intelligent and interested in the job by nodding, smiling and employing facial expressions at appropriate moments. An interview is a combination of self-promotion and ingratiation. Try to present the most positive of your qualities, and try to work out what the interviewers are looking for and how to show them that you can offer it. The most helpful facial expressions are a concentrated gaze, sympathetic nods to indicate appreciation of points being made to you, and alert, lively eye movements. If you believe they are looking for someone with initiative and flair, speak up and attract the attention of the interviewers. There will be more about the best mouth for having 'the gift of the gab' later in this chapter.

DO NOT: Fidget with your hair, tug at your beard or twiddle your moustache, pull your ear lobes, or play with your earrings. All these acts are commonly and sometimes unknowingly committed by people who are nervous or trying to make a good impression. Rubbing your eyes or touching your nose and mouth are also nervous gestures, but you ought to resist the temptation because each is a well known sign to an experienced face watcher that you could be telling lies, half-truths, or giving out misleading information.

nervous gesture

DO NOT: Apply a lot of make-up, after-shave or perfume unless you are applying for a stage role, or a vacancy for a model in a fashion house. A serious job applicant even in those careers should evoke the sweet smell of success, not the stale smell or tacky appearance that lavishly applied beauty products can create.

There now follows a number of qualities and defects which affect an individual's suitability for employment. This facial guide includes many of the qualities that are required for leadership, and will be of assistance both to those who want to consider what their own career aptitudes may be, and to those who have the responsibility for signing on recruits or choosing candidates for promotion.

Determination

You can tell if a person is determined and capable of completing a project, scheme, idea, plan or task by looking at the ears, eyebrows and mouth. Among the most telling are the ear's inner circle (anti-helix) and the helix, or outer circle or rim of the ear.

An extremely determined man or woman will have an inner circle which is raised higher than the helix (see page 85). In addition, the helix will be smoothly rounded, well-developed, springy, and free of bumps, notches or other blemishes.

A face in which the widest part is across the cheekbones is a positive indication of willpower, resolution, and its owner will have a strong desire to achieve tasks and targets. Furthermore, determined never to be outdone in trials of willpower and assiduity are those proud to boast of maintaining, whatever the situation, a 'stiff upper lip'. This facial attitude is best described as a pursed smile that is frozen, or rendered motionless, by an orbicular, or circular, clamp.

Unless you have taken time out to study your face closely you are probably unaware how deep or shallow your philtrum is. The philtrum is the channel that links the base of the nose to the top of the upper lip. A deep philtrum contributes to firmness and determination, both indispensable requisites for going places jobwise.

In the popular mind, strength and toughness are associated with those whose jaws are square, as exemplified by Winston Churchill. It is probably right to make this link, but to a personnel officer there are additional features of the chin and jaw which reveal the presence or absence of will and resoluteness.

Especially motivated to succeed in whatever they set their minds to are all those endowed with a protruding chin, which, whether square or rounded, represents a driving force to turn all opportunities to personal advantage. Notable among the great driving forces to have such a forceful chin have been John F. Kennedy, Jacqueline Kennedy Onassis, Pablo Picasso and many of the faces that feature in Picasso's paintings and sculptures.

protruding chin

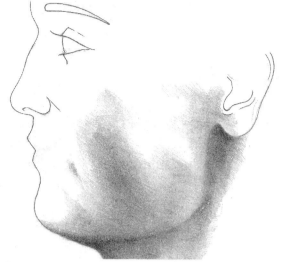

wide, deep jaw

A protruding chin is also a sign of arrogance, but who better to succeed in politics, big business or any profession where competitiveness is the norm than someone loaded with unstinting belief in himself or herself?

I have noticed in many Latin countries that men and women with wide and deep jaws – that is, plunging deep below the ear – are sought after by employers as sales representatives. For those with a wide, deep jaw are slow to tire, are tenacious, practical and persevering, and will not give up easily, all of which are greatly desirable qualities for a successful sales career.

Further facial indications of zeal and resolve are:

- Indented pulse points on the forehead (locate the two points by moving your index fingers along each side of the forehead above the temples until you feel the pulse beats).
- Rectangular-shaped eyes (which are also associated with cunning and slyness).

rectangular-shaped
eye

- Neat, orderly eyebrows which, if they are also straight, thick, long and flexible, reveal intense stamina and a will to succeed.
- Visible eyebrow roots (most eyebrows are either too thick or grow in such a way as to conceal the roots).
- Horizontal line(s) across the bridge of the nose, or between the eyebrows, or both. This is, moreover, a sign of obstinacy.
- A Roman nose: a high, prominent bridge which protrudes like a shelf.

Roman nose

If a man or woman has many of these facial characteristics he or she will, or should, go to the top of his or her profession.

Gaining recognition

There are many who are confident and determined to make a go of anything asked of them, yet power and success elude them. Anyone with a big mouth is inclined to overcome problems by externalising and airing them noisily. In an argument, for instance, a big-mouthed person will often make a lot of fuss, and become quite overwhelming, putting down the opposition with jests, insults and often hurtful comments. Minutes later, they cannot recall what they have said, and are amazed to find others withdrawing, in conversation or even emotionally, from them.

If those with large mouths are unable to curb their tongues, they run the risk of alienating those in a position to recommend their advancement. Big-mouthed men and women are frequently suited to the entertainment industry, where their wayward mouths and vivacity can be seen and used to advantage.

The small-mouthed have an equally tough time gaining recognition. They tend to bottle up their problems, unable or unwilling to confide in others. By the time they pluck up courage to open their mouths, the problem has most likely been solved and the credit gone to a rival employee.

When employers are looking for leadership qualities they are likely to discriminate against those who have baby faces. Rather than employ anyone with large eyes, plump cheeks, and a small nose and chin in a high status job, they prefer mature-faced candidates with thick eyebrows, small eyes, high cheekbones, and a broad chin.

Dr Leslie Zebrowitz, a researcher at Brandeis University in Massachusetts, who has made a study of baby faces, reports that baby-faced people suffer job discrimination like other minorities.

To an onlooker, those with flat cheeks appear self-confident, firm and resolute, but these men and women are, more often than not, quite timid. Suited primarily to creative work, they ought not to look for a career which requires teamwork or 'we're all in this together' attitudes. Rather, being more reflective than spontaneous, they work best alone and at their own pace.

Some people have a lot of ideas and suggestions, but lose interest before implementing them. Builders and construction workers are notorious for this inability; loath to see a job through, many vanish – probably to another job – before finishing yours. Another example is the travel agent, who eagerly proposes to a client a three-week visit to China, Hong Kong and Bangkok, gives an overall quote for the vacation, but fails to send the tickets and itinerary.

You are warned from doing business with this type of unreliable man or woman by the type of eyebrows they have. Neat at the beginning (closest to the nose), the hairs then proceed to splay untidily from around the middle of the eyebrow, before finishing in a jumble of disordered ends.

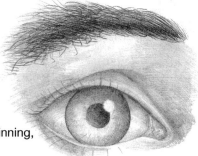

eyebrow neat at beginning,
then untidy

Unreliable, under-powered, and easily overwhelmed are those limited by modest personal resources. For example, unable to concentrate long enough to solve a problem, they react tensely and tersely, thereby clouding their judgement and foresight.

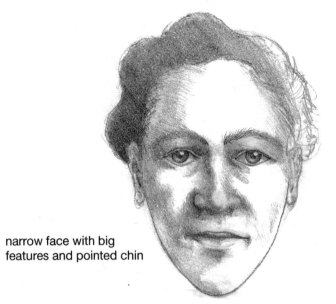

narrow face with big
features and pointed chin

Anyone with a narrow face and big (or biggish) eyes, nose and mouth will have this shortcoming, and should not look for employment which requires much personal initiative. They should seek work which does not require long periods of concentration. Working in a bank or financial institution would not suit them, nor would any position requiring charm, discretion, reliability and good customer relations. So, if you are in a hurry to check out of your hotel, pay the bill, and get away in time to catch a plane or train, do not expect prompt, efficient service with a smile from a receptionist or cashier who has a narrow face and big features. The condition is exacerbated if the face is oval-shaped or the chin tapers to a point.

There are certain facial traits that are indicative of faint-heartedness and lack of toughness. Anyone having two or more of the following list of facial attributes ought to be strictly supervised at work, though guided rather than dominated in order 'to get the best out of them' by making full use of their talents:

- an acutely receding chin;
- a narrow, curving jaw (that is, steeply angled towards the ear);
- mouth corners that turn steeply down;
- a soft, mushy mouth that is almost always partly open;

soft, mushy, partly opened mouth

- eyes with a permanently drunken or sleepy gaze;
- small, thin ears;
- a snub nose (see page 61); and
- a very thin or threadbare beard.

threadbare beard

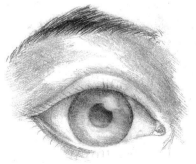

Decisiveness

If you are unlucky and work with colleagues who cannot make up their minds, who change the rules as they go along, indecisive and in two minds about everything, you will know the meaning of stress.

Indecision is a familiar and trying phenomenon at all levels in the workplace, so colleagues and employers are likely to place a premium on the abilities of those who are capable of taking decisions and sticking to them.

There are unlimited opportunities to practise 'spot the decisive decision makers'. You can do it, for example, while you wait in line at a bank or post office, if you have lunch or spend the tea break alone in the canteen, or on the bus or train that is taking you to work. Here are the facial features to look for in the face of a decisive person:

- Very pointed, triangular eyebrows belong to an acutely decisive person. Ho Chi Minh, the Vietnamese political leader, had eyebrows like these.

triangular eyebrow

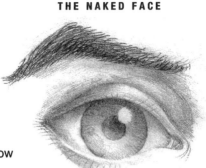

boomerang eyebrow

- Boomerang-shaped eyebrows like Ayatollah Khomeini's.
- Slanting forehead (an *acutely* angled or sloping forehead is a sign, however, of impulsiveness).
- A broad, square jaw is suited to a job where action and initiative count. A broad, rounded jaw belongs to a marginally less decisive person; this man or woman is gentler and kinder than one with a square chin and jawline.

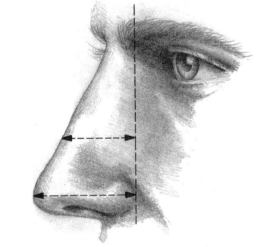

big, high nose

- A big, high nose is associated with those quick to make decisions, for whom the maxim, 'he who hesitates is lost' has intense meaning. A high nose is one which has high 'sides' topped by a prominent ridge.
- A mole on the chin in the C position. (See the mole chart on page 155.)

You have probably come across a lot of people at your workplace who make a habit of answering a question with the response: 'Yes and no'. They are frustrating to have to work with, unless of course you are the culprit yourself.

Ditherers, waverers, and the undecided seem to see-saw, shuffle, and oscillate their way through the work-day, and you can be forgiven for wondering why some of them got their jobs in the first place. You will probably never know, but if you scrutinise their faces and learn to recognise the shilly-shallier, you might, in later years, make more appropriate appointments to jobs requiring competence and decisiveness if you reach executive rank on your own merits.

A number of telltale signs reveal the vacillators:

- Anyone with a flat nose lacks spontaneity in reactions, preferring to take time to mull things over. They are slow to make a decision, subscribers to the 'look before you leap' brigade of workers.
- Those with babylike foreheads which protrude across the top zone (or the area immediately below the hairline) tend to intellectualise even simple situations, conditions and events, paralysing their decision-making processes. It is as though too many thoughts and ideas flood in to clog up their powers of logic and reason. These are the type of people who will give a brilliant answer to a question concerning the future of the Japanese Yen on the world's money markets, but tie themselves in knots if you ask in which room the committee should meet.
- If the forehead is much longer than the middle zone (from the eyebrows to the nose tip) this would suggest chronic indecision and defeatism (see page 33).

Authority

Those with authority can exercise their status and power in a number of ways. They might terrorise their staff and colleagues, or they could use their power to reward and reassure. The ways they do that could be as simple as leaving open the office door so that there is instant access for members of staff, or giving an encouraging smile or nod of approval when praise is due.

Then there are the 'experts', looked up to by their colleagues or subordinates as powerful people with special knowledge, qualifications or ability. Or, there is the 'proper authority', 'governor' or 'boss' believed by others to be the only, or best, person authorised to make decisions.

The terrormonger will use his face as often as his voice to frighten or punish: frowning, tightly pursed lips of sour disapproval, angry glints or a spying, all-seeing gaze, all of which can create a disagreeable atmosphere in the workplace.

Authority based on reward and respect for others does not require constant observation of the workforce, but coercion does. Workers might do the necessary (though often it will be no more than the minimum of work) while they are being surveyed, but will easily lapse into their old ways when the pressure of detection is off.

An individual destined to attain a position of authority needs to have a fair share of assertiveness, persuasive skills, shrewdness, ambition to influence other people, and the ability to recognise a good worker. A competent face reader can see whether a person has any of these qualities.

An assertive man or woman copes with all-comers, in any circumstances or event. The muscles under the corners of a forceful mouth are well-developed, and can be seen moving or twitching while their owner assesses a situation before giving his verdict or issuing a command.

The reverse is also true: a flat or hollow area below the corners of the mouth signals inability to stand up to aggressive people, but those who recognise this weakness in themselves are likely to strike out in unpredictable ways, releasing pent-up anger or, more rarely, latent violence. Any suppressed anger or violence is exacerbated if there are deep indents or dimples in this position. For instance, Colonel Gaddafi of Libya has small indents below the corners of the mouth.

indents below
mouth corners

Dominant people can signal their control over others by a powerful gaze and a non-smiling expression coupled with what is popularly known as a lowered brow: a stern, unyielding frown. Lowered brows are identified not only with assertive behaviour, but are exercised to express anger or deep concentration if someone is engaged in competitive tasks.

The command of attention is a reliable guide to knowing a person's status in the workplace. If someone enters another's office and 'forces' the other to look up quickly, he has higher status. The longer the second person takes to look up, the greater is *his* status.

You are probably familiar with the situation in which a man or woman is on the telephone when someone enters the room and proceeds to stand over and gaze hard at the person making the call. The weaker of the two will give in; even if the subordinate is making a perfectly legitimate telephone call related to the job, he will end the conversation quickly or say, 'I'll call you back' to the person on the other end of the line, and will immediately look at his superior's face to receive his orders.

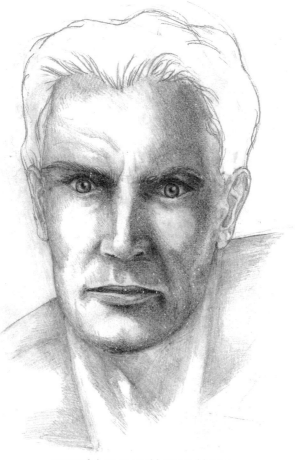

powerful gaze and lowered brow

When two people are conversing, you can generally see who is the dominant one. Their face, head and voice are raised authoritatively at the end of a question, and their eyes open wider. To signal 'don't interrupt me because I haven't finished speaking', the face and head of the dominant person remain straight, and their eyes stay fixed and unflinching until they are ready to continue. These are simple gestures made by the face, in particular by the eyes, but very telling if you can detect them.

You can count on the chin to tell you about power, glory and authority. And there are no surprises: certain to be more dominant than most are those with markedly protruding chins and anyone with a deep, wide, square chin. Able to impose their will, they expect and get others to obey, serve or agree with them. It should come as no surprise, either, to learn that anyone with a powerful chin is usually selfish and egotistic.

Look, too, to the cheekbones and cheeks to gauge authority:

- high fleshy cheekbones — inclined to use authority with fairness

- high, bony cheekbones — tempted to use their authority for personal gain

- high cheekbones with a depressed area between their highest point and nose — likes acting alone; generally uncooperative; lacks team spirit

- low-set cheekbones (when the highest part of the cheekbone is on a lower level than the middle of the nose ridge) — lacks authority; cannot expect to rise to the top echelons at work

As low-set cheekbones reveal a lack of authority, so too do ears that are disproportionately large for the size of the face. Men and women with very big ears are usually liked and readily helped, but despite the advantages and opportunities that come their way, they find it difficult to grasp and hold on to power.

Small ears or a thin, 'bony' nose are associated with modesty and insignificance, and are a feature of individuals ever-ready to put themselves down. They are self-effacing and apologetic. If you accidentally knock them over in the street when running to catch a bus, or you spilt hot coffee over them, they would probably say 'I'm sorry'. For what, you might wonder? Easily overwhelmed by others, and often totally lacking self-confidence, it would be cruel to give them great responsibility. Unfortunately, this fear of responsibility is more apparent if the ears are also flat, pressed close against the side of the head and face.

Lack of authority and influence are evident from some facial expressions and gestures. Frequent blushing or lowering of the eyes to avoid your gaze are two factors of which to be aware. Moreover, anxiety is present if a person smiles, nods, blinks, or utters 'yes, yes' too eagerly or at the 'wrong' or inappropriate times. These frequent interruptions signal, 'I'm here, please notice me' or, 'Yes, I couldn't agree with you more', suggesting a need to be at the hub of things. But these are powerless people, unable to make an impression or influence events and decisions.

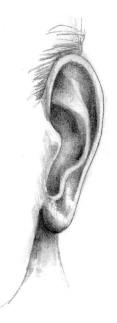

small, flat ear

There is an unusual facial clue that permits you to identify someone lacking persistence, initiative and influence: a mole in the natural beauty spot position on the highest part of the cheekbone (see the mole chart on page 155).

There are ways and means of discovering who is the dominant and the subordinate person in any relationship or situation. We have already seen the facial attitudes struck when a strongman or strongwoman enters the room or office of an inferior. In anger, the dominant person might thrust his face forward, glare at the other, and bark out an order, almost baring his teeth. The weaker one looks away, only daring to glance back in order to detect a change of mood or gauge the other person's next move.

A patently subordinate person such as a beggar, or employee seeking something he knows is unlikely to be granted, might screw up his face or make himself as faceless, insignificant and small as possible. Someone who is praying, or has just lost a competition or sports event, or is 'caught' in the act of doing something he knows is not right, will make his head, face, shoulders and back appear as small or short as possible.

Add to this an anxious facial expression, and you have a common re-action of a motorist stopped for speeding by a policeman, or an employee caught sneaking back late from lunch. By contrast, the dominant one stands tall, head and face are erect, and the gaze confident.

Face reading can help you to avoid irritating your superiors or colleagues. For instance, if their head is bent over the desk, eyes focused in concentration on an open file, this is not the moment to interrupt. It is equally important to know when to beat the retreat, when your presence is no longer desirable.

If an employee does not recognise another person's signals for 'that's all for now', he risks his superior's irritation, which might be bluntly expressed in a brush-off such as, 'Sorry, but I have to make a phone call now' or, 'Can we leave this for another time?' The employee is angry with himself for not having recognised the brush-off signals evident on the face of the superior before they could be verbalised.

The signals to watch for are:

- the other person avoids or terminates eye contact;
- a raised eyebrow to signal impatience or 'That's all for now';
- a slight twist of head and face in a look of doubt;
- a glance at a clock or a watch;
- looking down at the desk/papers/files/hands; and
- pursed lips and distracted comments.

These signals constitute face language for 'I've had enough of this for the time being', at which point you should have got the message that it is time to go.

Cunning and canny

It takes a certain degree of shrewdness and cunning to succeed at work, and even more to hang on after you have climbed to the top of the executive ladder. A canny person will not rest on his laurels, never underestimating the powerful driving forces which make others want to take his or her place.

People whose ears are long are particularly shrewd. A long ear is one where either the top reaches above eyebrow level, or the lobe drops below nose tip level. A person with an instinct for developing relationships with the 'right' people and able, through their position and influence, to help with promotion, introductions and advancement, will often have both features of long ears. Additionally, a long, supple lobe that hangs free from the cheek tells a face watcher that this individual is alert and usually able to anticipate a major problem before it arises.

A Roman nose is one with a high, prominent bridge, and those endowed with this certainly have a nose for business matters, their skills in negotiating and transacting deals proving to be great bonuses.

Teeth which slope inwards are never going to win a beauty contest for their owner, but they are not to be under-valued, representing as they do a sly, artful, resourceful individual well able to do battle with all-comers.

Slow and steady wins the race. Such a cunning, patient plan enabled the tortoise to triumph over the hare. The victor probably had small eyes,

bucket face

too, being a tortoise, and a face shaped like a bucket, for both facial characteristics belong to steady, orderly minded individuals who carefully weigh their options before taking a decision which is likely to affect their future.

Look around the office or your place of work, or at your friends, neighbours and family to find that those with small eyes are astute, alert, wily and, occasionally, ingenious. Some will be distinctly deceitful, given the opportunity or right conditions.

As to the bucket-shaped face, in Chapter 7 you will see that anyone with this shape of face is alert to being used or taken advantage of, by others. This face shape also symbolises a strong will and ability to influence others. The present Pope, Picasso and Luciano Pavarotti are distinguished by bucket-shaped faces.

Ambition

Unless you were born into a greatly advantaged household, the one true way to get the most out of your career and work is to aim higher than the estimate of your potential made while you were still at school. Other than this goal, being able to read faces will give you a head start over colleagues attempting to get to the top without your knowledge of face reading.

Among the most ambitious are those with comparatively large ears, remarkable for having a prominent inner circle (anti-helix) and a well-built tragus (the bump or notch situated immediately above the ear lobe and beside the cheek. See page 116). The inner circle is the thick, circular section which usually runs briefly parallel to the outer rim (helix).

Ambitious men and women are rarely vain or self-satisfied. They have no time to be, for they are constantly searching for ways of self-betterment. A protruding mouth, in particular one in which the philtrum slopes acutely outwards is an instantly recognisable facial sign of someone who sets very high standards of personal behaviour. To live with someone like this necessarily means keeping up with their elevated standards, otherwise you risk incurring their displeasure and criticism. This can greatly strain a close, personal relationship or marriage (see page 107).

Enterprising, too, but with ambition limited to achieving one prime goal in life are the owners of a protruding lower lip. Here, the lower lip appears to hang down because it is, in fact, the upper chin or area immediately below the mouth which recedes (see page 128).

A great many under-achievers strive hard to succeed, trying till it hurts, their brave efforts thwarted by restricted talent. Many set themselves targets of achievement far beyond their abilities. Some blame themselves for failure, using up reserves of energy to fight off the inevitable. They then lack fighting spirit when it is most needed.

The face is an open book if you are searching for evidence to corroborate any suspicion you may have that a person's ambition exceeds his or her competence. For example, those with a wide gap between the eye and mid-eyebrow (more than an inch and a half) will see their hopes for promotion to a top job dashed unless they are lucky on the day of the interview by getting the 'right' questions and saying the 'right' things. As with examination papers this can happen, but most of us cannot expect to be lucky every time we have an interview for a job vacancy or promotion.

Other facial clues that will reveal to the perceptive interviewer the candidates least likely to do a good job because their ambition exceeds their competence or qualifications for the job in question are:

- one eye higher than the other;
- one eyebrow higher than the other;
- a mole in the middle of the helix (outer rim) of the ear;
- the nose is thickest in the middle when it is viewed from the front. This also suggests stubbornness; and
- a nose bridge that is narrow, shallow, concave.

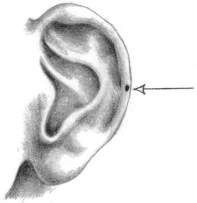

mole in middle of helix

70

Choosing a team

In times of high unemployment one would expect employers to be able to pick and choose the best from an enormous labour pool. Yet, even in favourable conditions employers still make mistakes, selecting weak and unsuitable candidates instead of the ideal people for the vacant jobs.

Even American presidents have problems filling the posts in their administrations. Chase Untermeyer, one of the executives responsible for making presidential appointments for George Bush from 1988 until 1991, reported a recurrent problem arising during the Cabinet selection period. 'He'll be OK for the job, but he'll need a strong deputy. After about the thirty-seventh time, I decided that what I needed was a box labelled "Strong Deputies" from which to pull a good match.'

Recognising the importance of 'pulling a good match' has led some American business enterprises to request a specimen of handwriting from applicants. This can be misleading, because canny job-seekers will make changes to their normal writing style in the specimen copy after first reading books about graphology. They would wish to conceal, for instance, any evidence of emotional instability, pessimism or dishonesty.

Reading faces is a more reliable way of spotting the good workers. The chart which follows will provide an at-a-glance guide to some of the principal qualities sought by employers in members of their workforce. The chart also includes some personal characteristics that might be useful to have in any case.

---

reliable; will do the job to the best of their ability, but lack initiative; better supervised than left to make decisions

rectangular forehead; horizontal hairline

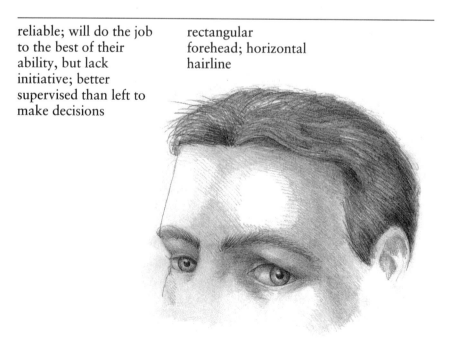

competent, good memory, has initiative, logical, very intelligent	wide, deep, rounded, smooth forehead; if the temples are hollow lacks energy
executive qualities; achiever	straight eyebrows

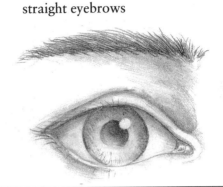

diligent; believes that a) God helps those who help themselves b) Stand on your own two feet c) Get on your bike and pedal to success	hairs grow vertically at beginning of eyebrow (area closest to bridge of nose)

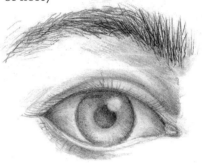

versatile, adaptable	flexible, supple, pliant eyebrows (which also indicate creativity)
practical	outer ear rim (helix) which is fleshy, thick, or prominent, or all three
impractical	small, thin ear lobes
clumsy; willing, well-meaning	short neck

would like responsibility, but a better employee than employer

steeply up-turning eyebrows

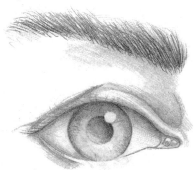

workaholic, worrier; extremely ambitious

deep vertical crease(s) between eyebrows;

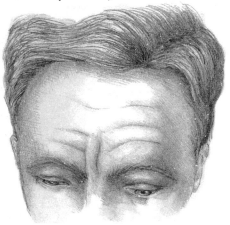

indented pulse points (side of forehead)

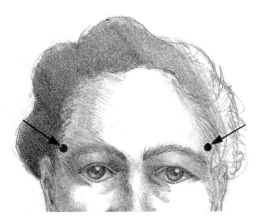

works hard at set-tasks, but can be stubborn	round eyes
they think about the job in hand; try to make the most of it	horizontal lines or furrows across the forehead; close lines suggest this person is mentally stretched by the work
an easy ride so far; rarely had to face problems	smooth forehead without lines or furrows (if over age thirty)
fighting spirit; tough; can cope with the unexpected	lower and upper lips aligned

loyal	wide nose bridge and eyes set wide apart
disloyal	crooked, pointed chin
has common sense	horizontal mouth corners joined by a straight line, visible when the mouth is closed

Battle of the sexes

If a woman has a problem of self-esteem, perhaps she should blame her face for it. A healthy, blooming face of an adult man is seen by his colleagues as representative of his competence. To them his face speaks of independence, activity, energy and competitiveness. His is the face of a financial provider, able to take the initiative inside and outside the workplace, day and night, on an equal footing with either sex.

However, a healthy, blooming face of an adult woman arouses the suspicion that she is overly concerned about her appearance, and likely to panic or respond with 'typical female' excitability in a crisis. So her blooming face prompts such typically sexist comments as 'Why don't you marry a rich man and give up this job?' or 'You're much too attractive to be a chairperson'. The sexist crushers or put-downers see her principal role as that of raising a family or cooking meals.

Worldwide, it is common practice for both men and women to look at a man's face first, but at the body of a woman before glancing at her face. In 1978 when groups of American college students were required to draw pictures of males and females, they gave more space to the faces of men, more to the bodies of women. Additionally, the men's faces were more accurately detailed while the faces assigned to the women were blurred.

In a nationwide survey among American male managers, women were rated as lower than men in skills, motivation and work habits, and they were deemed less able to make decisions or cope with stressful situations. Furthermore, it was considered acceptable for a man to be autocratic, but definitely not so for a woman.

In the late Eighties, a prominent American head-hunting organisation appointed to its London office an Oxford graduate in divinity to recruit the highest flying executives for British industry and commerce.

Barely reaching five feet in stocking feet, hair pulled back into a severe bun, granny spectacles riding low on the ridge of the nose, she was usually mistaken for the secretary by the majority of candidates, many of whom undermined their chances of getting the job by treating the formidable face-watching head hunter as 'a mere secretary'. If they had met her gaze, or acknowledged her presence with a smile, they might be higher up the executive ladder today. As you cannot judge a book by its cover, neither can you know a person without taking the trouble to study the face.

Achievement

Everyone loves a winner – or at least envies him. Tom Lehrer, the successful American humorist, once observed how sobering it had been for him to admit that when Mozart was his age, Mozart had already been dead for a year!

According to sociologists, the rich and educated put success down to hard work, intelligence, and good money management; the 'working classes' believe that it is ruthlessness, privilege in the form of inherited wealth or educational advantages that count, or that tax systems favour the rich, while at the same time 'the system' creates inequality and injustice.

Moreover, sociologists in the industrial nations find that the middle and privileged classes attribute failure to lack of ability, unwillingness or inability to adapt to new conditions, or say that 'They don't try hard enough to get on in life'.

Their findings concerning the unemployed and chronic failures are that those who deem themselves unsuccessful look upon their failure as the result of bad government policies, inefficient management, bad luck (such as illness), world recession, or the introduction of automation.

There is a type of forehead which reveals who should not try to make a career in business. The forehead with no business brain behind it is small, narrow, bumpy and indented. Anyone with this type of forehead should not employ others, nor should they even think of starting up their own business. There is an exception. The disadvantages of having an unbusinesslike forehead are mitigated if the person has a determined chin, one which is square (or smoothly rounded), deep and protruding.

Chinese experts in face reading have advice for shopkeepers, sales personnel, airline staff, hotel and office receptionists, and anyone hoping to make a successful career in public relations and the professions which bring them into contact with a large number of people. An unsmiling man or woman should not be employed in such jobs because their bitter faces will frighten away the customers.

Whether you make a success or failure of a job depends in part on how you cope with the complexity of it. If it is too easy and you are not mentally challenged or stretched by what you have to do, you will be quite considerably depressed by the end of the working week. However, if you find it a struggle to keep up with the demands of your job, your degree of depression and frustration is likely to be even more acute. Chapter 8 describes the facial clues for identifying stress in an individual. It should be repeated here that stress arising from work can lead to bad judgement and accidents.

An important source of stress occurs when a person takes on too much, through unwillingness or fear of relying on others to do the job properly. Individuals who are unable or loath to delegate work or responsibility because they distrust others have, as distinguishing facial characteristics, either deep indents or dimples at the corners of the mouth, or a diamond-shaped face (narrow forehead, widest across the cheekbones, narrow or pointed chin).

indents at corners
of the mouth

However, those whose faces show the presence of both characteristics
– that is, a diamond-shaped face with *deep* indents in the mouth corners –
can count themselves among the rare individuals who overcome all ob-
stacles to reach the top of their chosen career. They are, given good health,
destined to fly high.

SPOTTING THE HIGH FLYER

Full marks go to the employer able to spot the up-and-coming high flyer.
A man or woman destined to go places will have a strong combination of
the good qualities described in this chapter, their faces amply revealing
their potential and merit to astute face watchers.

For Henry Ford, the question 'Who ought to be boss?' was like asking,
'Who ought to be the tenor in the quartet?' To which his answer was: 'Obviously, the man who can sing tenor.'

The 'tenor' could be the president of a country or company, the com-
mander of the armed forces, the elected jury foreman, or the captain of the
local darts team, but whoever they are, all leaders need articulate skills to
be able to establish a winner's identity.

Whether they work in policy-making which affects the national interest or in a lesser capacity in a small business, they will need to be
intelligent, but not too bright. As it has been noted by C.A. Gibb in 1969,
there is evidence to suggest that although every increment of intelligence
might mean wiser government, nevertheless, most people prefer to be
badly governed by leaders they can understand.

There are others at the top who think more like Samuel Goldwyn: 'I
don't want any yes-men around me. I want everybody to tell me the truth
even if it costs them their jobs.'

Potential leaders do the most talking in group discussions, and their
opinions prevail. Their facial gestures and expressions compel others to
notice and listen to them. You will be aware of one outstanding member
at a dinner party or a meeting who, by a powerful gaze or a way with
words, wins everyone's attention.

A man or woman endowed with leadership skills can make others jump to obey when they issue a command in the form of a question. 'Would you like to eat now?' seems simple enough, but if the question issues from the lips of a leader, it will be taken as a command that now is the time to start the meal.

A command-question goes with raised eyebrows and the leader's nose will most likely point the way to the door, table, or wherever it is he wants you to go. He or she is, in effect, leading you by the nose.

The nose reveals a lot more about a person's instinct for leadership. Obviously, a big, wide, solid nose with a high central ridge and fleshy, evenly shaped sides to support dilated or generous nostrils will allow the free flow of air to enter the nose, supplying energy to lungs and bloodstream. On the other hand, pinched nostrils and above them flat, eroded sides are more likely to produce anxiety and untidy decision-making.

There is yet more about the nose than meets the eye: if you can identify the right nose you will be looking at the best planner and organiser in your company or corporation.

The best nose a leader can have is a large one, but you should be aware when you are looking for the high flyers that men's noses are bigger than women's. The female high flyer will not require as large a nose as her male counterpart, but will be advantaged if her nose is larger than those of other women.

convex mid-nose ridge	foresight; good concentration
convex mid-nose ridge, low bridge and plump, fleshy sides (of nose); prominent superciliary ridge	a success story: the best organiser-strategist; able to direct all ranks of employees; intuitive; calculating

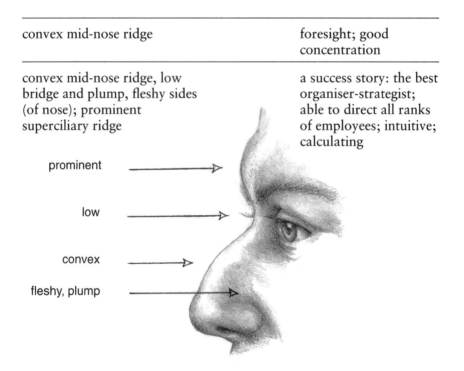

prominent ⟶

low ⟶

convex ⟶

fleshy, plump ⟶

aquiline nose	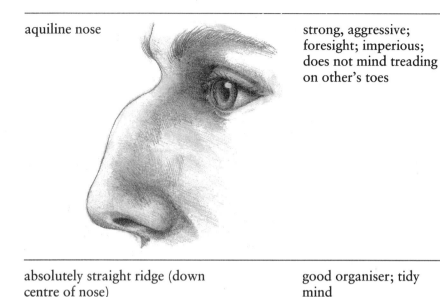	strong, aggressive; foresight; imperious; does not mind treading on other's toes
absolutely straight ridge (down centre of nose)		good organiser; tidy mind
downward-plunging, very long nose		good negotiator; a 'head' for business affairs; tends to put own interests first

Authoritative and decisive men and women of action usually have sharply delineated mouths, often with highly coloured lips, or, if they are black, lips which are well-defined and glossy.

Action is not everything, though. Top leaders are also required to know when to adapt, negotiate or compromise. They need to understand that compromise is not necessarily a sign of failure, and that not all negotiations have to be a test of power. It takes considerable judgement to be able to assess situations accurately and see what the circumstances require.

The face can reveal whether or not a person possesses the necessary judgement to be able to achieve a leader's balanced viewpoint at work and the ability to direct relationships with the workforce successfully.

Look for eyebrows which slope immediately up from the bridge of the nose (the bridge ought to be quite high, quite wide, and straight) for a sign of good judgement. If, however, the eyebrow levels out in the middle-growth area, instead of continuing in an ascending arc, this would immediately suggest gullibility, not a plus point for someone being considered for a job at the top of a profession.

There is nothing like charisma for making your mark in politics, showbusiness, and many fields of leadership. There is no agreement on what makes some of us charismatic or what causes some people to be attracted so powerfully to others. Whatever charisma might be, it can be sensed almost like a magnetic field across the face.

Conjure up the image of one or two individuals whom you would consider charismatic; their faces will contain or put to use one or more of these signals:

- extensive use of facial expressions and movements to emphasise a point.
- active or exaggerated lip movements to attract the viewer's attention. These facial devices are normally alternated with changes of pitch and loudness of voice, or by changing the rhythm of speech.
- a strong, compelling, power-packed gaze levelled at the audience or television cameras at the end of a speech, interview or statement. Or, if the charismatic man or woman has only you as the audience, the compelling gaze is for you alone.

Good eye contact is part of the face-to-face armoury of the giants of big business. In many countries, when a business deal is being negotiated it is vital to hold the gaze of the other party if the deal is to be successfully concluded and a contract signed. This is a good practice in South Korea, Taiwan, Hong Kong, China, Europe, Russia, Australia, New Zealand, South Africa, Argentina, Bolivia and Chile. In North America the confidently held eye contact is usually followed by a firm handshake between the business parties. It should be noted too that to many Americans no eye contact represents boredom or a lack of interest in those present at the time. Establishing visual dominance to relay power and status is rated high among leadership abilities.

Top-flight business executives, academics, media people, and leaders in a multitude of organisations do well for themselves and the society or enterprise they represent in Asian nations such as Japan, China, Korea, the Philippines, and especially Thailand, by not talking or laughing loudly in the presence of their hosts or the men and women with whom they hope to do business.

In Thailand it is especially important to know that you should never touch the face or head of another person, for touching the face of a Thai man or woman is taboo.

High flyers can come to little harm anywhere if they are armed with the gift of the gab. Naturally, you will look to the mouth to reveal whether or not someone has this gift. There are three factors to look for, and the more you have the greater your accomplishments are likely to be. They are:

- a deeply curved lower lip.

- a gradual slope from centre of lower lip into the upper chin.
- lower lip corners that are smooth and flat.

Do you have the gift of the gab? If you have the 'right' mouth or answer 'yes' to most of the following questions, you do.

- Can you speak about anything and nothing on demand and at all times?
- Can you charm and hold the attention of others?
- Would you describe yourself as being instinctive and physical rather than intellectual?
- Is your logic generally overtaken by passion or sensuality?
- Do you like the sound of your own voice?
- Do you have a lot of bare-faced cheek? For instance, would you agree with J. Paul Getty that it might be all right for the meek to inherit the earth, but certainly not its mineral rights?

And, finally, there is, according to a great number of Vietnamese and Chinese experts in the art of face reading, one rare facial characteristic which reveals to the world the identity of the greatest leader of all. This unique man or woman has four whites in the eye: above and below the iris and pupil, and on either side of the iris or coloured areas. The eye is like an island surrounded by a sea of white. Industry, trade and commerce would probably benefit by having some with 'four whites' in top jobs, but this type of eye is rare, and so we are denied the services of these extremely talented men and women.

CHAPTER 7

LOVE AND FRIENDSHIP

Everyone needs friends. It is choosing the right ones that is difficult. Most people have as friends those whose company they find pleasing and agreeable, and count themselves lucky if their friends are good-looking, outgoing types.

But friends are most valuable, and even necessary, in times of trouble, when we need someone to turn to for help, sympathetic understanding, good advice and possibly even a solution to our problems. Congenial companions of the past may prove fair-weather friends at times like these, and the facial features of the people who will prove to be friends in need may not relate at all to conventional ideas of good looks and 'friendly' features.

Few people are in a position to choose friends solely by face-reading. Friendships develop mostly at work, among neighbours, through common interests such as politics, sport and music, or are inherited from childhood or school. Few friendships last a lifetime.

This chapter explains how the face can tell you more about your friends and loved ones, the affection in which they hold you, and their strengths and weaknesses. The face is a helpful guide to gauging the value and closeness of your friendships.

You can make an assessment of the closeness of a relationship between two people by observing the distance they keep between their faces. Less than eighteen inches is the usual intimate distance between lovers' faces; friends' faces are generally kept between eighteen inches to four feet apart, while the formal distance between business associates or acquaintances is normally more than four feet. Couples who are sexually attracted are inclined to put their faces close to each other.

Research and observation have identified that women are more tolerant of facial proximity than men. Pairs of women will position their faces more closely together than two men with equally warm feelings of friend-

18 inches

18 inches to four feet

four feet or more

ship. Furthermore, Arabs, Latin Americans and Southern Europeans are happier in a close face-to-face meeting or encounter than the English, North Americans or Swedes, all of whom prefer to keep their faces further removed from each other.

The unwritten rules concerning personal space can be seen in operation when people feel that someone is getting too close. Feeling tense, anxious, or threatened, they will pull back their face from the intruder, or momentarily close their eyes, or tuck their chin into the chest, thereby signalling, 'Don't come any nearer because this eyeball-to-eyeball situation is getting too close for comfort.'

We like as friends those who are similar to ourselves. They agree with our ideas, seeing eye to eye, as it were. They bolster our confidence in the correctness of our outlook and actions; it is unpleasant to be challenged, criticised, slapped down or squashed. We like our friends for the feeling of well-being and familiarity they bring us, as so aptly described by Professor Higgins in the musical, *My Fair Lady*, when he admits to missing Eliza's face which had become as familiar to him as breathing in and out.

If people like you they look at you while listening to what you have to say. It is worth noting, however, that American research has shown that black people tend to look less when they are listening to someone. This knowledge will help to avoid misunderstandings at work or in personal relationships, and contribute towards a more harmonious atmosphere in the office, other workplace, or clubroom.

Few of us can resist liking the friend who listens attentively and copies our own facial expressions. An example of this mirror-image practice is the expression of alarm or concern on a friend's face, mimicking our own facial expressions when we are distressed or angered. Equally, friends smile with pleasure to reflect our own when we receive good news.

HOT AND COLD

Some people are warm, others distinctly chilly and reserved. There is a popular saying that the face of a frigid person would crack if he or she tried to smile.

Warm and friendly people develop smile lines radiating from the outer corners of the eyes, rather like the sun's rays. However, if these lines already appear on the face of those under the age of thirty, the face will age prematurely, appearing in later life years older than the owner's true age.

Warm and good at human relationships are those endowed with a broad, round chin (especially if it is also short) or anyone with an attractively fleshy, plump nose tip. Their warm and friendly spirit is further enhanced if the nostrils are generously wide and rounded.

The inner circle (anti-helix) of the ear tells us whether a person is uptight and reserved, in which case it is flat and undeveloped. A 'friendly'

broad, round, short
chin; plump nose tip

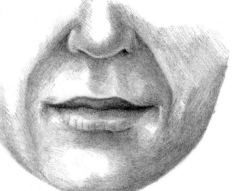

prominent anti-helix (inner circle)

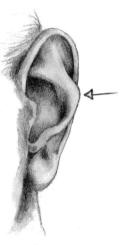

inner circle – prominent, high, thick and developed – singles out those whom you will find friendly, easy-going and approachable.

Cold people are critical, spending much of their time disparaging other people, events and situations. It is commonly believed that thin-lipped people are cold, and this is largely true, but a more reliable telltale sign is the nose. Those with a narrow nose tip pointed like a beak easily have their noses put out of joint, and are likely to have a penchant for nit-picking.

Another quick to take offence is the owner of a thin, angular, hard-looking nose. If this person can also stare at you and hold your gaze without displaying a flicker of a smile, you are looking into the eyes of a very cold and unfriendly man or woman.

Another giveaway to a chilly type is the presence of a flat area between the upper eyelid and the eyebrows, almost giving the appearance of a lack of flesh here. These people have put up a protective wall around themselves. It is terrible to fall in love or have a close relationship with someone as chilly as this, because you will feel hurt, unappreciated and unloved. You will never, or hardly ever, get beyond the protective barrier; the barrier will cause considerable anxiety.

Two further pointers to a chilly disposition are: prominent high cheekbones accompanied by a very pointed chin, and a marked disinclination to having the face touched. In the latter case, these cold people almost certainly suffered from a lack of loving touch and caresses when they were very young, thereby inhibiting their ability to relate to others. Unable to express warmth in relationships, they cringe at the prospect of getting a kiss, or peck, on the cheek.

Sociable, friendly people have a good middle zone (the region between eyebrows and nose tip), which means it is longer than either the top zone (above the eyebrows) or the low zone (nose tip to bottom of chin. See page 33). For them, making and keeping friendships is important. By contrast, someone whose forehead (top zone) is longer than either one of the other regions is cerebral, often introverted, and finds developing close personal relationships a problem.

Protruding eyes signal sociability and gossip-gathering, so you would be wise not to reveal your secrets to their owner.

It is easy to make contact with people with big, generous mouths. They tend to be good conversationalists, knowing a little about most things, with the possible exception of science and money management. However, they are somewhat superficial, busying themselves with personal news concerning people, places and events.

big mouth with
pointed corners

Now, if the big, generous mouth also has pointed corners this person is immensely sociable, loves chatting and may frequently tell little 'white' lies in order to spin a good yarn. Normally uncritical of others, these friendly people rarely stop to think about what motivates them.

Plump, generous cheeks or a smoothly rounded hairline are further evidence of easy, approachable amicability. By contrast, someone whose hairline comes to a V-point in the middle of the forehead may well try to be a friendly, warm person, but the chances are he or she has to pay to make or keep friends. These friendly people will invite friends to dinner, the theatre, concerts or even on holiday, giving more than they receive in return. They are over-eager and try too hard and often to please.

There is no immediately apparent reason why someone whose central forehead is shiny should be popular, but observe well and you will notice that many of your best-liked colleagues or friends have a fine sheen in the middle of their foreheads. Another to enjoy this distinction of popularity is the person (it is usually a woman) whose nose tip is slender and refined.

IN OR OUT

To be, or not to be, an introvert or an extrovert? For the most part we have no choice, for either we are spirited, outgoing, enthusiastic, and self-assured, or we are not. We can identify from the face the type to which most people belong.

Generally speaking, introverts have eyes that slope down, their mouths are small, and their cheeks are flat. Conversely, extroverts have eyes sloping up, bigger mouths and fuller, plumper cheeks than those of introverts.

Extroverts hold your gaze more often and longer while introverts position their faces further away when they converse, keeping their eyes down more often, too. A reliable indication is that introverts have a longer top zone than low zone while the reverse is true for the extrovert. There is a simple explanation: the top zone contains the brain and the low zone includes the mouth.

Extrovert or introvert, you will have greater reserves of inner strength and willpower in your relationships with others if your face is bucket-shaped (see page 69).

It is difficult to be a good listener. We can listen to about 650 words per minute. On average we speak about 150 words per minute, leaving a lot of time for the listener to think, assess or daydream. Good listeners are likely to be good friends because they are interested in you. A bad listener is not a good communicator, the mind and ears are closed to you and to what you have to say.

The best communicators have dominant middle zones in the ear, that is, the central part is longer than either the top or lower zone. If the middle zone is very short this indicates that its owner is preoccupied with his own welfare, and is certainly a bad listener. (See page 37.)

The ear is a wonderful provider of information, though few will have studied their own ears. Moreover, no two ears are the same, even on the same head. Like fingerprints, the ear is strictly individual and could provide police forces with an alternative identity check on criminals.

Take a look at your own helix, the rim that runs along the outer edge of the ear. If yours is wide or robust you are inquisitive and like eavesdropping on other people's conversations. You will read a newspaper over the shoulder of a fellow passenger on the train or bus and will always want to find out what other people are up to.

If your helix curls over and forms a little tube or pipeline you are more cranky and idiosyncratic than most.

curled helix

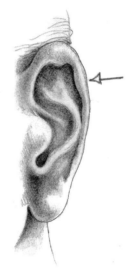

Mean or generous

On the whole, it is easier to like someone who is generous and a bearer of gifts than a penny-pinching meanie. The face lends itself to a quick and easy generosity test devised about 3500 years ago by the Chinese. It is advisable to look into a mirror while you do this test.

The test consists of three quick movements to one of your own ears:

- Grasp an earlobe between your index finger and thumb.
- Run the index finger up the lobe until it rests on the U-shaped notch at the top of the lobe.
- Lightly rest the index finger in the notch. If it is a tight fit (that is, the notch is narrow) you are mean, not at all generous with money, and you are a calculating person. If the notch is wide and the index finger has plenty of room to move around, you are generous (with money, possessions, and your time, patience and concern for others).

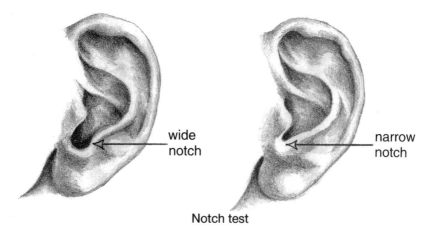

Notch test

Slightly more suspect is the beard test to measure generosity. The beard of a generous man will not grow right up to his lower lip. If it does, its owner reflects the characteristic of his beard: the beard locks up the mouth to prevent acts of generosity from getting out. Moreover, a generous man will be able to grow a moustache that covers the philtrum, but a mean man will have skin left bare in the philtrum no matter how hard he tries to cultivate a full beard and moustache. Hairy tales? Doubtless they are, but true.

There is another mean-generous test: anyone whose top and lower lips are both full and fleshy is generous.

Bores, Boring

We often pardon those who bore us, but never those whom we bore. True grit from the pen of the remarkably observant French writer La Rochefoucauld.

If you take time out to notice the face of someone bored by your presence or conversation, you will see their zombie-like, glazed stare washed perhaps by the tears of a suppressed yawn. Or the hapless victim will stare blankly into space, or cover up those near-to-dropping tears by rapid blinking. It is possible to bore people to tears.

Those with round, baby-like faces are easily bored. But whatever the face shape, a bored face will nod and move in unusual patterns as the owner tries to stay awake while the friend or relation or colleague talks. Another sign of boredom is the eyes looking round the room hopefully or hopelessly, depending on the level of frustration.

It is unfriendly to inflict boredom on another. You can see you are doing it if your victim starts nodding or smiling (with the lips but never the eyes) at wrong and inappropriate moments, for instance, if the person you are addressing nods or smiles while you describe the agonising day you spent in the dentist's chair or how you felt during treatment for sore knees while 'under Dr Jones'.

A bored person will probably keep his or her face towards you, but the body will be turned in another direction, poised to escape at the first possible opportunity. Bored listeners might prop up their face in their hands. You will detect your success at reawakening their interest and attention if their face becomes erect and alert, or face and head are tilted or cocked to one side in readiness to receive what you have to say.

A misfit is one who misses out on simple exchanges of ideas, who wants to make his or her presence felt but cannot quite tell when to intervene and when to hold back. These people have no sense of timing, and they find themselves excluded from conversation, relegated to the role of a person without importance, bearing or influence. A common facial characteristic of the misfit is a protruding lower lip.

Yours sincerely

Sincere, kind, compassionate, trustworthy, open, good-humoured, with a sense of humour, and he or she keeps promises. What more could you want in a friend? It is easy to judge our friends and find them lacking and not the 'good friend' we thought they were. We do not hear from them for ages, they forget we told them about our accident or bad health, or a problem with a second son, or that the dog got run over and the new one bit the neighbour's leg and the whole unhappy incident got into the local paper.

Other friends may try to make excuses for 'not calling you because we've been so busy and Henry has been looking for a new job, but I meant to ring you to ask how you are.'

Do they really have any concern for you, or is their professed friendship insincere? Is their explanation truthful, or are they, too, lacking in sincerity?

The face reveals whether or not someone is sincere. A mouth with clearly defined lips, the outline of which appears to have been inked in with a fine pen, is an important indicator of a person's sincere intentions. If there is, in addition, a perfectly straight line where the top and lower lips meet you will find as sincere a friend as you could hope to have.

An insincere person is good at those 'flash' smiles lasting less than a second. They need not have bothered because in that split fraction of time the energy spent serves rather to chill you than to provide any hint of warmth or sincerity.

A cordial, but unfelt and therefore not a genuine laugh has the same effect. The laugh dies prematurely, stopping suddenly, taking itself by surprise. Expressions of insincere appreciation tumble out of the mouth, sometimes mimed, often *sotto voce*.

Those who are insincere in most of their dealings with people have no difficulty bringing their faces back to neutrality after an insincere, polite smile or laugh. Of course that does not debar you from choosing them as friends. Oscar Wilde said, 'A little sincerity is a dangerous thing, and a great deal of it is absolutely fatal'. But then his tastes were rather special.

Kindness and compassion can be seen in the eyes. If you tell an anguished story about being made redundant, for example, or how you had to borrow money to buy a special gift for a very sick or troubled wife, the eyes of a compassionate friend will be directed on your face with close attention, the eye contact rarely wavering or wandering. This is likely to be accompanied by audible expressions of concern through pursed lips, or the sympathetic listeners will bite their bottom lip, frown (near-parallel, vertical lines up the middle of the forehead), and they might shake their head. A female listener may be moved to tears, a male reduced to unsteadily flickering eyelids. It is all part of 'feeling for others'.

It is not uncommon for men and women with protruding eyes, unhappily called pop-eyed, to be endowed with a huge capacity of fellow feeling for the sufferings of others. It is as if these eyes can say: 'I know how you feel', or 'I wish I could do more than just listen to you, unable to do anything to help'.

However, if the eyes that speak here of concern are dry rather than moist, hard-staring instead of 'soft', you are, alas, listening to superficial expressions of compassion, and insincere ones, too.

Many kind people have round ears – but remember that round ears with tiny lobes denote much less attractive character traits: this man or woman is stubborn and considers material comforts more important than most things in life.

KINDNESS

We all like to have our acts of kindness acknowledged. It is an unpleasant fact that the people most likely to ignore you after you have held a door open to let them pass are those with thin lips and frosty eyes. It is far less likely that one will be upset in this way by those who have a convex bump in the middle of the nose ridge because they themselves are usually friendly and appreciative (see illustration on page 92).

The best way to cope with such commonplace gestures of unkindness is to have a sense of humour. No one likes a perpetually sour-faced person. The only thing you risk losing when you laugh is a straight face.

A person with a sense of fun has a glint in the eyes. The dead-pan look in the eyes and faces of the Hollywood comics in the famous movies of the

bump on ridge

silent era were put-up jobs; a witty man or woman does not have lustre-less, uncommunicative eyes.

People with broad, round, short chins are noteworthy for their good humour and openness. Easy-going people can often be distinguished by their flattish nose bridge, the type of nose that cannot hold up spectacles or reading-glasses, with the result that its owner puts down the spectacles and seems to be forever searching for them. Because they are relaxed and easy-going, at least they do not get excessively annoyed about it.

TRUSTWORTHY? FICKLE?

How can you know whom to trust?

People with flat cheeks or those with mouth corners that curve smoothly upwards are open and predominantly honest. However, they do not readily let you see into the workings of their own thought processes, plans or schemes. Rather, their openness concerns you; they will tell you what they think about things that affect you.

People with broad, square chins see themselves as trustworthy, though a wise man or woman would look to these square-chinned wonders for a relatively light, uncomplicated friendship with no demands or high hopes expected from either party. Do not place too much faith in them.

Another facial pointer of which to be wary is the nose with a nose tip that turns down towards the mouth. This person cannot be trusted any more than can the person with a combination of two factors: a very thin lower lip and a shifty, watery, weak gaze.

Fickleness is a principal cause of decline in a friendship. Women will be aware of once-happy friendships with other women who let the relationship disappear as soon as an attractive man turns up in their lives. But when the man disappears as quickly as he entered the life of the ex-friend, the chances are that the ex-friend will be in contact with her old friends again, suggesting 'we must see each other again after such a long time.'

Who are these fickle beings? The facial signs to look for pertain to male and female faces, and they include: a rounded hairline sweeping smoothly across a curved forehead; curly eyebrows (see page 45); teeth that are narrow or very thin; and small foreheads. And one other not to be missed is the person who looks at your companion or the person you are with, hardly sparing you a look. Or, the fickle one could only have eyes for you, ignoring the presence or very existence of others you are with. The attention that these people give you is inclined to be short-lived if they set their sights on a newcomer, one endowed with greater appeal than even you.

There is one other possible explanation for the 'fickle' look: that the person has fallen in love at first sight and cannot take their eyes off the newly adored one. So how can we tell?

Love

In an ideal relationship both partners would love each other equally, but most love relationships are lopsided with one loving the other more. Many would privately admit to preferring to be the loved one than the one whose love for the partner exceeds the love shown them.

The upper lip reveals our capacity to love, the lower lip shows how much we need to be loved.

Bigger upper lip
Loving, but not needing to be loved. Attracted to extra-marital affairs.

Bigger lower lip
Need for love exceeds ability to love.

A person with lips of the same size and width, or one whose eyes are wide (each eye more than one and a half inches from side to side) is able to give and receive affection in about equal amounts, which is very satisfactory in a warm, friendly, loving relationship.

There are many ways of loving, the most intense of which is passionate love. Although the experiences can be wonderful for the lovers themselves, displays of their ardent feelings can cause envy, resentment or disgust in others. Naturally, many of the outward signs of passionate love concern the face.

Love at first sight is rare, but if it happens it is usually men who fall rapidly in love. Couples who love each other passionately are preoccupied with the loved one. 'We can't stop ourselves' is expressed by an intense mutual gaze of rapt adoration and a need to put their faces close together, all the better for nibbling the facial parts that stick out such as ears and the nose.

The partners give each other 'knowing looks' and lovesick glances enough to make a jealous or out-of-love friend green with envy. Some of the looks exchanged between the couple radiate the message 'You are perfect in every way'.

Men and women in love spend a lot of time looking into each other's eyes, with females looking longer and more often than males. The face muscles are taut, the eyes clear and brighter than normal. The pupils dilate (see page 175), and one or both will look away if intimacy is becoming too strong.

When the couple is apart the partners are likely to daydream, and concentration suffers, particularly if the relationship is running into trouble. You may have noticed how a colleague's work suffers when he or she feels insecure in a love relationship. For example, concentration wanders, or he or she will remain in the office during the lunch break, hoping for a call; appointments are forgotten, and tempers are short.

The eyes cannot conceal unhappiness. A rejected lover pleads with the eyes if he or she hopes for a reinstatement of a failed or failing relationship, but the desperate look usually irritates. There is something totally unappealing about the hangdog eyes of a rejected lover.

You need look no further than the eyes to learn a lot more about another's love problems. Those with deep-set eyes, for instance (see page 134), are inhibited and cannot easily show their feelings. This is tough on the partner, and gives rise to the often-heard complaint that 'he or she doesn't understand me'.

Round eyes signal frankness and a penchant for plain-talking, which can be a positive factor in some relationships, but misplaced in the delicate business of love, where tightly controlled emotions are easily upset.

round eye

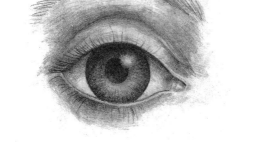

More disappointments can be expected from the person whose heavy eyelids droop over the eyes (see page 124), an indication that this individual craves affection and attention. To be involved with this man or woman can be emotionally draining, physically demanding, and cause considerable anxiety.

As passionate love tends to be intense, fragile and short-lived, many prefer the calm satisfaction and happiness in companionate love where, gone hopefully, are the rapid swings between highs and lows, elation and troughs of despair implicit in ardent, feverish relationships. In passionate love the face is too often the mirror of unhappy and unattractive emotions and reactions: anger, black looks, frowns, 'hurt' expressions, tears, sulky pouts, frustration and anxiety.

Companionate love consists largely of affection for the one with whom one's life is deeply entwined. Here, there is time for being like 'best friends'.

Companions in love still engage in long eye contact, but now the gaze is to check on the needs of the other, to monitor the other's well-being or welfare.

One facial sign of a pessimist is for the eyes to slope down, but this facial feature also identifies someone able to love another for what he or she is, rather than what the lover hopes for or expects.

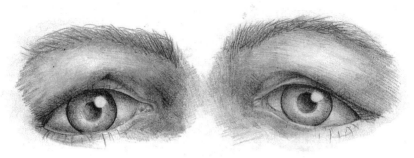

eyes slope down

This characteristic of the eyes may imply a touch of pessimism, but at least the owner will not nag. In countless marriage surveys conducted in the United States and the United Kingdom, the majority of respondents have listed 'nagging' as one of the most common causes of breakdowns in marriage.

Plump, moist, red lips (shiny for black lips) signal a warm-hearted, affectionate person. Add to these plump, full cheeks and twinkling eyes and the total makes a very pleasant companion. If the eyes incline upwards, this is an optimist who sees the best in others (and you), is hopeful of the joys the future can bring, and he or she will seem years younger than their real age.

A word of caution, however; if the eyes slope steeply up in excess of forty-five degrees, their owner is charming but cunning and possibly dishonest.

FOREVER AND EVER

How can one identify someone with whom a marriage can be built to last? A valuable prerequisite is a rosebud-shaped mouth. People whose lips are reminiscent of a rose in bud are romantic and dreamy.

Now look closely at a person's upper lip. Most will have a dip at the centre of the top of the upper lip, called the point of refinement. When

point of refinement

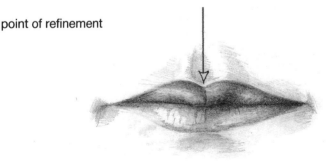

there is a perceptible vertical line joining this point to the bottom of the upper lip its possesser will not only be romantic, but refined and delicately creative in love as well.

And if, at the bottom of that vertical line, the upper lip has a downward point (called the point of sensitivity), then this person really will make a wonderful partner for life.

point of sensitivity

In fact, if someone is endowed with a point of sensitivity, the chances are good that he or she will be a faithful, kind and devoted partner.

Those with large eyes (which are wide from the upper lid to the lower lid) are slow to commit themselves to another, protesting the good life of freedom is preferable to being tied down to domesticity.

Those with active eyes that sweep the scene before them with an all-embracing glance are quick to declare that they are willing to commit themselves, but are soon off again in search of the good life. These are the eyes of the roving, unsettled types, exuberant, worldly, extrovert and good fun as companions, but not as companions for life. The man or woman with the roving eye uses others for sexual satisfaction. If you can accept this and take this person at face value you will have a lot of pleasure, but if you are looking for a long-term partner this is not the one for you.

Sentimental are those with very small, slightly sunken eyes. Since 1860, research in Britain and France has also shown that many of us have a slight quint. If it is present in the left eye, the researchers say this is a pointer to sentimentality and hypersensitivity. Gullible, easily duped and much too trusting are those with eyebrows that rise steeply at the beginning.

While we can never know what surprises life can bring there comes a time for most to want a quiet life free from financial strain, employment worries, and domestic battles on the home front.

If you want a well-organised home life, arranged by an orderly partner who likes to handle matters skilfully, you will consider committing yourself to someone with generously wide, round nostrils. This person may be precise, practical, even bossy, but you and others will never be bored.

In addition, if the area between the eyebrow and upper lid is fleshy, this indicates that its owner is capable of giving himself whole-heartedly to family, friends, causes and events, such as fund-raising for a charity.

Many people marry someone whose face resembles someone else from their past. Although many of us are attracted to unusual or exotic faces or types, most eventually settle for a partner who is from a familiar background.

Someone boasting that they adopt the stiff-upper-lip attitude associated with straight-laced British army officers can be counted upon to honour the monarch or president, home and family, at least by outward appearances. You must consult Chapter 9 if you wish to know what this type of person might get up to when the stiff upper lip is ever loosened.

Another to give family values pride of place is someone whose eyes are round, clear and big like cows' eyes.

The family member who values peace at all costs, and sidesteps the first sign of trouble is the one with a very flat nose bridge. For this man or woman is easy-going, at times subservient, and can be dominated and bullied by family relations and friends. This is most likely the weakest member of the family unit, and it is too bad if he or she is also the breadwinner.

Those with noticeably protruding or lopsided ears (where one is bigger than the other) generally contribute in a major way to family discord and disharmony. So well is it known that the ears of Prince Charles stick out and that the left ear is bigger than the right, it should be no surprise that his home life was unhappy and apparently bleak. The message then is that prince or princess, housewife or superstar, man or woman, rich or poor, young or old, you must read assiduously the face of the man or woman with whom you are planning to spend a lifetime, before you opt for marriage.

CHAPTER 8

Sex, Strength and Health

There is absolutely no proof that the size of a man's sex organ is related to the size of his nose. Nor can the widely held fable that it is, be blamed on an old wives' tale because there are quite a number of old women who would thumb their noses at the suggestion.

Yet, by skilfully scanning the faces of others, paying particular attention to the eyes, mouth, even ears, and indeed the nose, you can assess their owner's sex drive, sensuality and whether he or she will be a thrilling, pleasing or hopeless lover.

Sex Drive

The first place to look at is the philtrum (the vertical groove linking the base of the nose to the upper lip). The wider the philtrum, the greater is the owner's sexual appetite.

On average, the philtrum measures a half-inch (just under three centimetres) at its widest point. Anything narrower than this indicates a modest appetite, while a wide philtrum suggests someone with a keen sex drive.

wide philtrum

receding upper lip

The lips also tell tales about a person's sexual needs. For instance someone whose upper lip protrudes very noticeably has to cope with a strong sex drive. An upper lip which slopes inwards provides intriguing information about its owner: these are people who are fascinated by and physically attracted to their own sex, although only the enlightened ones would admit to this.

Anyone with a fleshy lower lip will seek physical pleasures in abundance, whereas a thin lower lip indicates few or limited desires.

With practice, the face watcher can discern a lot about the sex life of others by looking for certain giveaway characteristics over which their owners have no control.

A man or woman with *intensely* green, blue or blue-green eyes has a frantic, creative sex appetite. If a single line emanates from the inner corner of either eye on the face of those under the age of thirty, these

three-dimensional chin

young men and women will have an enormous sex drive, which will almost certainly interfere with their concentration at work and their career. Similarly, those with a three-dimensional, fleshy circle in the centre of the chin will most definitely put sexual pleasures at the top of their list of 'Things I Like Doing Best'.

More than most, these three-dimensionally chinned wonders suffer from the fear of failing to make a success of close relationships. Many Don Juans have a three-dimensional chin and, fearful of failing to deliver the goods, they flit from woman to woman, so avoiding close personal encounters and accountability.

A clever observer can identify those with an insatiable sex drive. There are two facial features to look for: first, a sex maniac has gleaming, beady eyes, which are immediately disconcerting because they seem to stare right through your clothes. Secondly, the whites of the eyes are scattered with tiny red dots. It is important to identify the presence of *dots* not lines, for red lines signal strain, general fatigue, or a high intake of fatty substances in the diet.

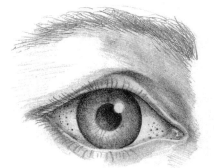

red dots in
whites of eye

A weak libido can also be detected from the face. A small nose is a pointer to a modest sex drive, and the appearance of a rash, blackheads or whiteheads on the nose is another sign of a reduced libido, though both the skin condition and the effect on the sex drive are probably only temporary.

IMPERFECT DESIRE

Everywhere there are people who cannot understand why their sex lives are unsatisfactory. They have partners whom they like or love, but at the very moment when pleasure and total fulfilment should be theirs, something happens to impinge on their enjoyment.

For instance, those with nose tips which turn down towards the mouth tend to be strongly sexed, but these are especially mean and selfish people, and they are frequently impatient with their partners. And so the pleasure principle is threatened for both partners and the libido is diminished.

Others to suffer the effects of strained libido are those whose lips are full, and joined by a wavy line when the mouth is in repose (see page 28). Their problem can be summed up in four words: 'No one understands me'. They too see their immense sex drive wither, their needs extinguished by self-pity.

Look to the ears, in particular the lobes, for another sure sign of sex blocks. Those with small lobes will definitely have exceedingly strong sex urges, but they seem to be driven by the need to give immense pleasure to their partners, so much so that they cannot relax and enjoy the experience for themselves.

On the other hand, someone with small lobes and a smooth, round outer rim to the ear will be too lusty for all but another with the same type of ear.

round ear, small lobe

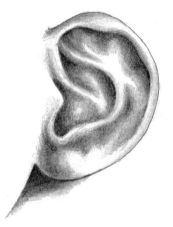

A powerful sex drive or a weak libido notwithstanding, anyone with an impaired sense of smell loses interest in sex. This may be because of some temporary indisposition such as a cold or hayfever, but those for whom sex is always little more than a nuisance or an infrequent pastime when there is nothing worth watching on television will include anyone who can never smell a gas leak or the dinner burning, or see the point of sniffing wine before drinking it.

YOURS SENSUALLY

Eyes that roam and linger over the body of others belong to a person alert to the pleasures of the senses. Their expression could be identified variously as being liquid, deep, dreamy, contemplative, penetrating. Or, most compelling of all, bedroom eyes.

Bedroom eyes are shiny, melting and persuasive. They are incredibly attractive sexually to someone of the opposite or the same sex, holding in their powerful gaze the promise of magical times.

bedroom eyes

Great lovers from the history books and screen idols from Hollywood are credited with possessing this attribute. However, if you are thinking of giving a loved one or a desired person a bedroom-beckoning look, remember that this gaze cannot be simulated or held more than fifteen seconds if it is not genuine.

Upward-slanting eyes are associated with sensuality. It is a look which many women try to achieve with cosmetics, in particular, eyeliner and eye shadow.

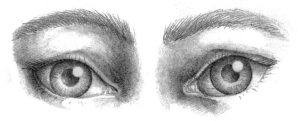

upward-slanting eyes

Two surefire pointers to unfiery lovers are 'bloodless' lips, which also go with a ruthless, cruel personality, and a drunken gaze (bleary and unfocused), which indicates that their owners are unreliable, living in an impenetrable dream world. Men and women with a drunken gaze are inevitably disappointing lovers because their partners never feel they really know them.

FLIRTING

To flirt, men and women use the face in a dazzling display of expression and gesture to attract attention. First, he must catch her eye, then he holds her gaze a little longer than usual, trying not to let her eyes slip away. Perhaps he will narrow his eyes (a glint) or raise one eyebrow, his eyes lingering on her throat before roaming down to her breasts with a gaze full of promise and sensuality. He moistens his lips, narrows his eyes (again), telling the woman by the look in his eyes, 'You are the one for me'. By now the woman is uneasy and excited.

It may read like a romantic novel, but this is the pattern in everyday life for a male in flirting mode or mood. Meanwhile, how does she respond, if he succeeds in arousing her?

There is a flicker of a smile playing about her lips. She may lower her eyes, even fluttering her eyelashes. The importance of eyelashes in sexual attraction is attested by the wide variety of false ones sold. They can be wispy, raggedy, in clusters, full thickness, half-thickness, in tassels, long or short, or alternating long and short.

The fluttering done, she peeps, thereby entering the ambivalent stage between flight and approach by turning away while at the same time looking at him. At this point she pouts, fiddles with her hair or brushes it off her face, tilting her head and face to one side. If she speaks her voice will be low and private, and possibly a bit breathless. Another romantic novel? No, more of the same, but this is the general conduct of a female in flirting mode.

Men and women do share certain facial expressions and gestures when they are flirting. They smile more and look more readily at different parts of the other's body. They tend to nod vigorously when agreeing with the other person, darting glances to check each other's reactions.

Driven by a conscious or unconscious desire to present themselves as readily accessible, like an open book, they keep their hands away from the face, for there is as yet no cover-up and nothing to hide. They will lick or moisten their lips from time to time, occasionally teasing their own top teeth with the tongue. If there is mutual attraction they will bring their faces close together in order to exclude any third party.

The next stage might be the little-girl kittenish approach or the little-boy lost appeal. To work on his protective instincts she will turn her widened eyes, open and appealing, towards him, or pout, or cock her head to one side. Maybe she wants him to feed her a spoonful of the ice cream he has just bought, or she will pop a pen or pencil into her mouth and suck the surrogate lollipop. This facial activity sounds and looks infantile, but flirting is a private activity not meant for the observer.

His little-boy lost tactics are consciously or unconsciously directed at arousing the maternal feelings of the woman he desires sexually. He will pull childish faces and speak with a childlike voice, saying a host of childish things. And he, too, derives pleasure by opening his mouth and closing his eyes, hoping perhaps to have pieces of popcorn popped into his mouth, or to get a kiss. Men and women of all ages may be observed in childlike displays of affection as long as they feel young at heart.

Gay couples engage in intensive eye contact when flirting; a man glances at another's crutch and away in a fraction of a second after eye contact has been established.

Generally speaking, hetero- or homosexual, we ignore the flirting gaze of a stranger if we do not want to develop a relationship, but return the look if we are interested.

Almost as universal as a taxi, the wink is a password for flirts around the world. Remember, though, if someone winks at you incessantly the chances are that it is a tic and its unfortunate owner has not even noticed you. As we say on at least five continents, that's life!

AROUSAL

And now for the key question: can you tell if someone is aroused or sexually stimulated by looking at their face? First look at the eyes.

When we are sexually aroused by something we see, the pupils of our eyes dilate. Tests carried out in the United States in the late Seventies showed that a man's pupils can widen to twice their normal size if he sees a naked woman or a photograph of a female nude.

The French writer Stendhal anticipated modern ways of communication when he remarked that women issued an invitation by a gaze because they could later deny the 'contract', as it could not be quoted.

The eyes impart more information if their owner is sexually stimulated. Shining or dewy eyes betoken tenderness. Eyes that gleam or glint tell of passion. And as we saw earlier in the section on sex drive, bedroom eyes signal, 'I'm ready'.

There is no doubting the readiness for action of the giver of the hard stare aflame with desire and conquest. This fiery stare is frequently accompanied by pelvic rolls or thrusts, a series of side-to-side wriggles and airborne heaves of pelvis and hips. Both men and women are liable to perform the movements, the rate and power of the hard stare and pelvic thrusts dependent upon the urgency of desire.

When a woman is sexually aroused, her lips, breasts and genitals swell as they fill with blood. By using lipstick, a woman mimics the moistened genitals of the sexually excited female. The lips (of men and women) are one of the most sensitive regions of the body, responding readily if the slightest touch is applied to this exciting erogenous zone; female lips are also larger and fleshier.

Where swelling and reddening of the lips is a sexual signal among the fair-skinned races, the equivalent response on a dark-skinned face is a quick quivering and swelling of the lips, depicting sexual arousal.

Flaring nostrils indicate sexual arousal and excitement, though they also frequently accompany an outburst of anger. In either case there is a reflex action in which the nostrils seem to curve or flare or widen upwards and outwards when the muscles stretch. Flaring nostrils are often accompanied by heavy breathing, especially when a person is sexually aroused when kissing.

The ear lobes also respond to erotic stimulation by tingling or becoming ticklish; many successful seducers get their way by nibbling the lobes of the desired one.

And, finally, here are four indicators that tell of a person's readiness for sex: the face muscles are tense, ready for the moment; the eyes get brighter; the man or woman will blush, go pale, or start to perspire freely. And good news for those over forty years of age: any bags under the eyes or facial jowls will seem to dwindle as you swing into action.

SEXUAL SATISFACTION

An experienced face watcher can assess whether or not a person enjoys love-making. For instance, most people who have a markedly protruding mouth are not easily satisfied sexually. Their inability to relax is often the result of strict parents or even stricter teachers at school, whose ideas about sex would have stressed the 'unwholesomeness' of sex, its 'sinfulness', or that it is 'dirty'. It may take a considerable effort over many years for a person with such a repressive upbringing to throw off the residual feelings of guilt every time sex for pleasure occurs.

Some people take a long time to reach a climax, and are even slower to give their partner a satisfying experience. They are distinguished by a long, thick upper lip. Dominated at times by a powerful sex drive, they are more concerned with self-gratification than sharing the experience with a

protruding mouth

partner. The delay in pleasure is deliberate for they seek ways and means most suited to their own sexual needs.

Others find sexual gratification quickly, among them the men and women whose mouths are small. Conversely, those with big mouths, though quickly roused, are more likely to suffer an uneven ebb and flow of desire, and are beaten to the winning post by their partner before they themselves have reached a climax.

As fast to the post as the small-mouthed are those with thin upper lips and anyone whose upper lip is shorter than the lower lip. But even their haste for satisfaction is bettered by the lucky ones who can abandon themselves totally to supreme desire and pleasure, the intensity of which most of us can only dream or read about.

short upper lip

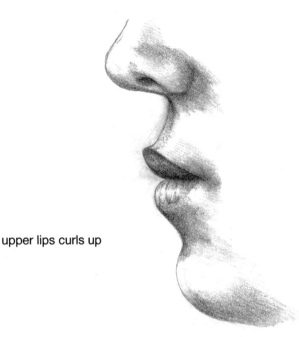

upper lips curls up

Who are these fortunate people, able to experience paradise on earth every (well, almost) time? They include those with a concave upper lip (which curls up); those whose upper lip is especially fleshy; someone with eyebrows which curve naturally like a new moon. If the new moons are

new moon eyebrow

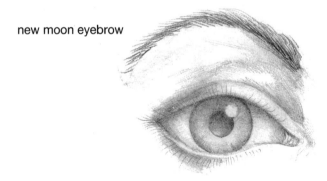

also thick their owner is capable of experiencing the most fantastic orgasm known to mankind. There is one other person able totally to abandon himself or herself in mind and body in the sex act: someone with a concave mid-nose. All these then are among the luckiest people in the world.

concave mid-ridge

WHEN IMAGINATION RUNS RIOT

Once again the owner of a small mouth rates well in the chart of imaginative, inventive lovers. Others who can be counted on to give their partners an ingenious time will have well-defined, clearly outlined lips. This applies in particular to black, brown and dark olive faces; the equivalent feature for white and pale skins is very red lips.

Another indication of a lover with novel but largely pleasant ideas is the presence of fleshy, plump, puffed ear lobes (see page 26). This person will crave close physical encounters, but is usually extremely patient, preferring to bide time until the 'right' sexual partner can be found.

Imaginative lovers can be crude or refined in technique and practice, and both kinds will find partners who enjoy what they have to offer.

upper lip curves
continuously

Crude, bestial, even brutal lovers can be identified by their mouths. For instance, someone whose upper lip arches in a continuous curve (instead of dipping down in the centre) is certainly uncouth. Violently

straight upper lip

passionate, rough but inventive in their sex ideas are those whose upper lip is straight, wide at the corners, and slightly puffy.

More bestial than most is the owner of an upper lip whose centre dips almost to the level of the lower lip. People with this lip easily lose self-control, their paroxysms either delighting or alarming their partner.

upper lip dips to
level of lower lip

The upper lip is also the clue to refinement and sensitivity in the creative lover, male or female. A distinct 'V' or sharp point in the middle of the upper lip is called the point of refinement, and whoever has one is most certainly a caring, sensitive and imaginative lover. There is, however, a minus point: anyone with a point of refinement is also timid and touchy in the everyday world outside the bedroom (see page 96).

Unsatisfactory Lovers

One man believed it was possible to tell from the face whether someone was an unsatisfactory lover. He is Muhammad Ibn Kamil al Misri, whose *Encyclopedia of Pleasure* remains one of the world's most outstanding works of erotic literature.

No personal details are known about the author, though it is likely he wrote from Baghdad, about 1000 years ago. Only three manuscripts of the encyclopedia have been found, all in Arabic, each priceless work now locked safely away from the 'wrong' eyes in Istanbul.

I can summarise two fascinating aspects from the encyclopedia: the first concerns unsatisfactory male lovers and the second shows that a woman's face can be a giveaway.

Unsatisfactory male lovers

• very rough, bushy beard	excessive seminal fluid
• big nose and wide nostrils	strong penis, but lacks stamina
• big nose and wide nostrils and nose tip pointing upwards	curved penis, which has no strength
• sunken cheeks and bump in middle of the nose	no stamina

A woman's face is a giveaway

• big mouth	wide vulva
• small mouth	narrow vulva
• very thick upper lip	thick labia; too much fluid
• very thick lower lip	thin labia; easily hurt in sex act
• red, thick tongue	dry vulva; easily hurt in sex act
• short chin and wide nostrils (nose)	deep vagina; not easily satisfied
• big face and thick neck	big vulva

In the eighth and ninth centuries in the Middle East it was fashionable for poets to pass their time in the souks and slave markets. Poets such as Al Jahiz or Al Ra'i noted the type of women who would give great pleasure to a man: the favourite appeared to be one whose facial skin was as smooth as a baby's buttocks and as soft as silk, for she would provide a man with unforgettable thrills by the way she moved and gyrated her hips during sexual intercourse.

ARE THEY HAVING AN AFFAIR?

It is not difficult for the experienced face watcher to work out who is having an affair.

The couple sit close together, drawing their faces as close as circumstances permit, and while they gaze intently at each other they are quite unaware of others. If they become separated because, for instance, one of them is called away to take a telephone call, their attempts to get together again as quickly as possible are followed by comfort behaviour, such as beaming smiles, a quiet nod, or one will blow a kiss, or stroke the other's nose.

Another example of uninhibited gestures (and we are assuming the lovers are still at a happy stage of the relationship) is the popular tweak on the loved one's nose or ear lobe. The couple will be seen to confide and share these physical intimacies when they are not especially bothered about others knowing about the affair, or if they think no one is observing them.

A personal communication system exists to express their feelings of intimacy. It includes 'knowing' looks, winks, nose gestures, and synchronised facial movements to mimic and show understanding of the partner's emotions of, say, joy or frustration or anger.

Unless the relationship is turning sour, the couple will praise and also criticise each other relatively freely 'for the good' of the other.

The clearest clue, of course, is when the two people look guilty when caught together in what might well be an innocent situation: for example, someone sees them together in a wine bar; or they are seen coming out of an empty office after the lunch break; or they are found 'loitering' by the fax machine, their faces close together while they are in deep conversation.

Acting guilty would include blushing, rearranging or fidgeting with the hair, and avoiding your gaze. There might well be a lot of throat-clearing as they try to cover their embarrassment.

At a party or a social event, the observant face watcher will note that after a quarrel, a couple (married or not) will act formally towards each other, and if they smile it will be forced with no teeth displayed. Most unmarried couples tend to stay together in a group situation, their eyes sweeping over the guests from time to time before glancing at their partner for reassurance.

There is no one definitive pointer as to who might have a proclivity toward sexual harassment, but throughout this book many clues are available for anyone wishing to identify emotions such as temper, jealousy, envy, optimism, or aggression, all of which play a part in engendering this troublesome behaviour. Bear in mind, too, that the perpetrator can be a man or a woman.

It is timely, however, to reveal what the Greek philosopher Aristotle saw in the face of an opportunist. He noted that people with an overhanging upper lip would grab every opportunity to satisfy their sexual needs. He probably made the acquaintance of the first sex-starved harasser of women from among the playboys of the Western world exactly 2357 years ago.

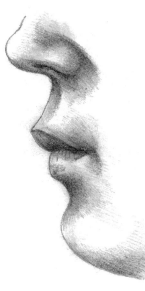

overhanging upper lip

A late twentieth-century diagnosis of a sexual harasser comes from Chinese sources: men and women whose eyes are shaped like new moons spend most of their waking hours in the pursuit of brief sexual encounters. For them every body of the other (or, in some instances, the same) sex is to be touched, explored and experienced. New moon eyes, then, are a facial feature of the sexual harasser.

new moon eye

ENERGY

If you want to ascertain how energetic or lethargic a person is, it is possible to find out at lightning speed by looking at their nose, chin, eyebrows and eyes in that order.

A plump, 'Roman' nose (see page 58) is associated with strength, energy and vitality, and is to be found on many of the world's wealthiest

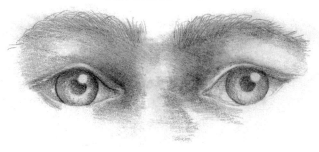

wide nose bridge

men (less often in women). Another nasal indicator of energy is a wide nose bridge which also tells of its owner's important reserves of strength; those with a wide nose bridge can greatly tire their sexual partners.

Moreover, a high or raised nose bridge means its owner can channel energy into attaining goals and ambitions, whereas a low or relatively flat nose bridge signals its owner's small reserves of energy and diminished achievement potential.

The concave or snub nose (see page 145) may be pert or cute on a female face, but it is in effect a weak nose, denoting a lack of energy and determination, even cowardice and passivity in both men and women.

Chins and jaws impart details of energy sources, too. Anyone with a straight or deep jaw (see page 57) tends to recover more rapidly after an illness than those whose jaws are steeply angled. Furthermore, many nervy, fragile people who are accident- or illness-prone, often have a narrow jaw.

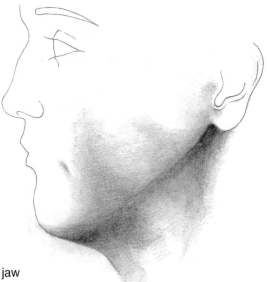

steeply angled jaw

As one might expect, a muscular jaw denotes great strength and vital forces, whereas a bony, fleshless jaw must obviously go with nervous debility, fatigue, and a lower resistance to illness.

Chins and necks provide a quick, ready-reckoner to personal strength and energy:

• short chin	uses up energy quickly
• wide chin	a sign of energy
• narrow chin	sporadic energy; excitable
• receding chin (often with a short jawline)	vulnerable
• a fleshy, circular area in mid-chin	strength, vitality, healthy sex drive
• pointed chin	lots of nervous energy, but unreliable
• long, wide, muscular neck	strong, energetic
• long, skinny neck	general fragility, but often adventurous
• long, skinny neck with a prominent Adam's apple	tense, nervy, irritable
• short neck	strong, sometimes clumsy
• short, thick, powerful neck	great strength, reserves of energy; can be brutal

Certain eyebrow formations reveal the extent of a person's energy. Thick, bushy eyebrows denote considerable strength, and many with these eyebrows succeed in their careers by employing bullying tactics, which seem to come to them naturally and effortlessly. If the eyebrows ride on a depressed bone, that is, sunken eyebrows, this is a good indication that this person lacks energy, tires easily, and needs a lot of sleep.

Further evidence of fatigue is discolouring in the whites of the eyes, generally seen as brown patches, or the temporary appearance of small red lines in the eye whites. While bright eyes speak of good health, energy and vitality, dull eyes, particularly if they are accompanied by a drooping upper eyelid, warn of diminished vitality and possibly of lethargy.

One final eye factor remains: very pointed eye corners (by the nose bridge) tell the world that their owner has limited reserves of strength and stamina.

You can never tell when it might be useful to discover whether or not a person is strong. You could be looking for a suitable companion to trek across Alaska, or you might want a partner who will not pop off at the first sneeze. To conclude this section on detecting strength from the face, there now follows a short list of facial characteristics to look out for. After this, there is a section devoted to assessing a person's general health by looking at the face.

Someone with a square-shaped face, with big eyes, nose and mouth will be ready to step into the breach in the event of trouble or danger. This person is indefatigable and energetic. However, beware the man or woman whose forehead is rectangular with hollow temples; this person lacks energy and could be a drag on your vitality and resources (physical and material).

Unexpectedly resilient are those whose cheeks are as flat as the great prairies of Canada. For these are courageous, independent people, unaware of their potential strength until they are called upon for help.

tragus

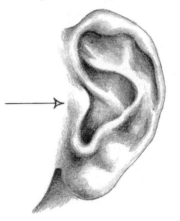

Vitality is a natural quality of those whose tragus (the little knob or bump at the entrance of the earhole under which any tufts of hair grow) is visible when you look at them straight in the face.

Naturally pale skin is generally associated with weak supplies of energy and determination. It is possible that applying pale powder to the face, especially the cheeks, is a womanly ruse to appear delicate.

HEALTHY, WEALTHY, OR WISE?

Stress can make us ill. Very ill. It suppresses the immune system. It is not uncommon for heart disease or ulcers to occur if there is stress at work, the result for instance of mismatching employees to the job either by giving them tasks that are beyond their capability, or by denying them the opportunity to stretch their mental or physical abilities.

Stress at work could be caused by something as small as a badly organised Filofax or piles of paper accumulating on the desktop, or there can be more serious causes, among them the threat of redundancy, job overload, such as working long hours or being besieged by phone calls, visitors and meetings. For senior staff there can be the stress of coping with pressure from superiors and the workforce, or taking the blame for others' misdemeanours and failures.

Many people work hard and ignore the signs of fatigue. They are concerned about controlling events, becoming over-anxious if they cannot get their way.

Stress can arise from any event or situation that requires people to adjust their ways or beliefs, make changes, or expend resources. On the whole we tend to under-estimate the angst that family reunions or holidays can cause if we ourselves are not affected by these events. Similarly, some of us will welcome an interview for a job as a challenge, even looking forward to the day, but others will feel threatened and insecure.

However, everyone suffers from some aspect of environmental stress, be it traffic jams, or a selfish neighbour or his barking dog, or a myriad of events and situations. Burn-out and emotional exhaustion can lead to withdrawal (from daily life and routine, work, the family and friends), depression, maybe alcoholism and, in severe cases, to suicide.

Of course, one cannot read in the face of everyone all the symptoms of stress, disease, illness and malaise to which they are subjected, but the face can provide clues and guidance in interpreting some of the problems.

If stress is induced suddenly by, for example, a loved one dying in an accident or trouble flaring up with the boss or mother-in-law, stress signs include quickening of the heartbeat (visible sometimes in the throbbing pulse points at the side of the forehead), beads of perspiration forming on the brow, or increased mouth and tongue movements because the mouth has gone dry.

If stress exists over a long period, brought on, for example, by marital separation, a major illness, losing one's job, or having to adjust to retirement from work, the facial signs might include a discolouration of the eye whites (either a yellowing or foggy look), small lip movements or quivers, excessive blinking and a host of eye tics. Tics range from flickering eyes (giving the impression of struggling to open and shut them simultaneously) to sticky eyes, wherein someone blinks but the eyes seem unable to prise themselves open quickly.

The eyes are a fair indication of stress. At times of difficulty people are likely to shut them tight, as if to block out unwelcome input from outside forces that pose a serious threat; the forces might be social, work, family, economic, illness, or just plain unwelcome. Many will close their eyes when they are appalled by a problem or upset by a friend.

Eye responses to stress are often accompanied by excessively frequent nods or noises of agreement to signal 'I'm listening to you'. The person appears distracted or unusually impatient, indicating stress.

A stressed person will frequently have difficulty meeting your gaze, preferring instead to glance rapidly away then back to your face while the conversation progresses. But as we have seen in Chapter 7, a shifty gaze can also indicate that people are lying or avoiding a confrontation, particularly if they are in the wrong.

Stress arising from having to make a decision between fight or flight is easy to detect for an experienced face watcher. The clues to look for are pallor, as the blood drains from the face, or a high flush (a response to excitement).

If a fight seems likely it is worth noting that the red-faced (flushed) person is less dangerous than the pallid-faced; if the pale face approaches angrily he is probably going to attack. The red face is less dangerous than he appears, because he is unnerved through waiting and the tension, which has been building up into a debilitating internal struggle, may fizzle out in shouts, oaths and curses. Nevertheless, one must be wary of an angry, red-faced, stressed person.

Some less acute stress signals are apparent if you take the time to study a person's face. No one can mistake the common face tics, which mostly take the form of grimaces, such as 'screwing up the nose' or twitchy, sideways mouth quivers, all rendered more serious if the stressed person also nods the head or throws it back in jerky movements.

If you are ever 'caught' watching a person's face and you are challenged for it, you could, circumstances permitting, offer your ideas for coping with stress.

The most obvious way is to remove or reduce the problem causing stress; or the sufferers might have to regulate their responses and emotions to the predicament by confronting or avoiding it. Being able to talk to someone who 'understands' could be the best way of finding a solution for the person under stress.

The American linguist, writer, editor and critic, H. L. Mencken cleverly assessed the respective roles of men and women. According to him, men got a much better deal out of life because they married later and died earlier than women. What he might not have known though is that both sexes can suffer mid-life tension, and that the face watcher can assess the extent of the problem by looking at the little groove, or channel, that runs vertically from the base of the nose to the middle of the upper lip.

This channel, or philtrum, tells the world who will suffer most from mid-life crises or self-doubts. Some will be bitter or rueful, envious or equable, but what they have in common is a feeling of having missed out on the best things in life.

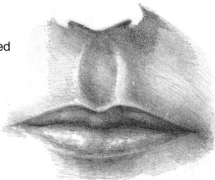

parenthesis-shaped
philtrum

The most susceptible to this loss of self-esteem in mid-life are the owners of a shallow philtrum, a crooked one, one with lines running across it, or a philtrum which bulges on the sides like parenthesis.

Whether you are rich or poor, plain or handsome, there are parts of your face which reveal your state of health.

Take indigestion as an example. A sign of digestive problems is a dry, scaly or mottled lower lip (which also is a giveaway to a person's suffering from constipation). Hollows in the lower parts of the cheeks are another symptom. So is teeth-grinding in sleep.

It is possible to identify those who suffer from indigestion by watching them while they eat. Many gulp down their food or eat when they are not hungry, after an argument with someone, for instance. Anxiety leads to bad eating habits, such as swallowing more air than normal. Over-eating is another contributory factor to indigestion.

A final thought about constipation, a condition which many find amusing until they experience it themselves: the people most likely to suffer this time-consuming discomfort are those with a very long, broad nose or anyone with a thick neck and a concave-curved nose. They should make sure to drink plenty of water and other liquids, and eat a high-fibre diet.

The face is also a remarkable indicator of kidney and bladder problems. Clue number one is the hair, noticeably a thinning out of eyebrow hairs and eyelashes.

Further signs of possible kidney or bladder worries are a slightly swollen face in which a small 'pit' remains after a finger has been pressed into the skin; recurrent puffiness of the eyelids (although this can sometimes occur in healthy people after a particularly long sleep); or wizened teeth surrounded by pale, shrivelled gums. Also at risk from kidney problems in middle-age are those with a small, receding chin, above which a deep hollow nestles immediately below the lower lip.

It is not only medical practitioners who can identify depression. Those interested in people can form their own diagnosis by analysing the face. Easy to detect are those who are in a persistently unhappy mood, or those whose concentration appears to have diminished suddenly. In Western nations, a depressed person feels inadequate, guilty or sinful. Their equivalent in India, Pakistan, Bangladesh or in Africa will feel tired and weak, and get frequent abdominal cramps; but all are likely to suffer from headaches, and lose interest in food, sex and social life.

Spotty or colourful noses tell the face watcher a lot about another person. A blue nose tip indicates pain in the abdomen, while a red nose tip suggests debility of the spleen, which lies in the abdominal cavity and plays an important part in the production of antibodies, which contribute to the body's resistance to infection.

The colour factor can be extended to the eyes. Red lines scattered in the whites of the eye reveal a high intake of fat in their owner's diet. The lines also warn against over-working, fatigue, and those who find they have them should slow down.

Most of us have two areas of white in the eyes: on either side of the iris. Some, though, have three or four areas of white – below the iris or, in the case of four whites, both above and below the iris in addition to white areas on either side. Three or four whites belong to those sensitive people able to sense something before it happens. But as they are also accident prone, care should be taken to heed these premonitions, even in such everyday situations as crossing a busy road or climbing a ladder.

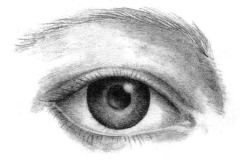

three whites

Ears have their telltale health signs, too. Those whose ears are thin will lack physical strength at times of stress over which they have limited or no control. Sufferers of gout will sometimes find crystal formations lodged in the fleshy rims of the ear; called *tophi lumps*, they are exacerbated by high-protein food.

Since 1989 researchers in Britain, America, Japan, Italy and the Republic of Ireland have been investigating a link between a certain type of ear lobe and heart disease. The British Heart Foundation has gathered the findings of the research teams, which indicate an association of a diagonal crease across the ear lobe at an angle of about forty-five degrees with heart disease, hypertension and diabetes.

If only we could get to see more tongues, for tongues are a superb indication of one's general well-being. A clean tongue without a coating denotes good health. Purple means stomach or intestinal disturbances or alcoholic toxins. Pale red warns of a deficiency of blood and vital energy. Think of anyone you know who frequently plays with the tongue, licking their lips and the corners of the mouth; this person is more peevish than most, and probably suffers from heartburn and bouts of flatulence.

LITTLE NUISANCES

The Spanish, Greeks and Italians believe our ability to survive a few minor ailments strengthens our resolve to combat a big one when it strikes. There are certain facial characteristics which a face reader can identify as belonging to those who get their fair share of illnesses and minor ailments.

The first characteristic is an acute slope between the forehead and the bridge of the nose. This is especially the case if the nose bridge is very narrow.

acute slope
between forehead
and nose bridge

A person with a small amount of hair growing on the nose bridge frequently suffers from minor ailments, many of them imaginary. He or she is likely to be a hypochondriac. However, thick hair growing here signals impatience and unpredictability.

ONE HUNDRED

Many centenarians have very large, thick ear lobes. Many have long teeth, in particular the two top central incisors, which are sometimes called tombstones. 'Long in the tooth' is a phrase one hears to describe an oldie.

One facial characteristic signals a very long life: if your philtrum (the vertical groove between the base of the nose and the upper lip) is at least one inch (about 5.5 cm) long you will live to a hundred.

CHAPTER 9

ECRETS

Some secrets are so secret that we forget to keep them. How undesirable it is, for instance, to let everyone know how jealous or envious we are, yet how hard to disguise.

There is much confusion about the distinction between these two emotions. *Jealousy* is the emotional response experienced when a person believes that someone else – real or imagined – poses a threat to a relationship. *Envy* is the feeling arising when one covets what someone else has.

'Anybody can sympathise with the sufferings of a friend, but it requires a very fine nature to sympathise with a friend's success,' Oscar Wilde observed, regarding the almost universal incidence of envy.

Transient envy can show in a darted look at a friend's huge diamond ring or a stunning new car, or it will express itself when a woman looks another up and down to see how well dressed she is.

Envy, then, can be detected from facial gestures. Otherwise, there are no other physical clues. Everyone is liable to be envious at some time.

Identifying jealousy is considerably easier for the face watcher. Jealousy is painful. 'Cruel as the grave', is how King Solomon described it, while to the poet John Dryden, jealousy was 'the jaundice of the soul'.

Jealousy is frequently linked to a low level of self-esteem, particularly if the person depends greatly on his or her partner as a source of self-confidence. Jealousy is felt, too, by women who are strongly dependent on a relationship with a partner when this affiliation is under threat. In such cases the woman believes the relationship is more desirable or rewarding than any available alternative.

Many men and women who are jealous by nature have either joining eyebrows or a generous growth of hair on the nose bridge, or maybe they have both hairy features. This copious growth of hair acts as a barrier to energy, thought and action, and so the jealous person's tormented

joining eyebrows

thoughts spin round and round in circles. Jealousy is a dizzying, oppressive emotion.

Charming, but only until the object of their desire slips from their grasp, are those with elliptical eyes, and in particular those with heavy lids, which allow relatively small areas of white to show on each side of the iris. These unfortunate people can be badly affected by the bouts of rage and insecurity that jealousy bestows.

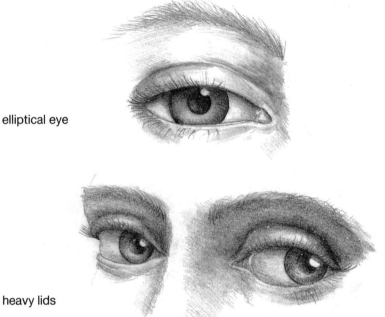

elliptical eye

heavy lids

Another clue to jealousy can be gleaned from the eyes; if both eyes feature irises which 'look' or appear to turn slightly inwards toward the nose, this condition reveals to the face reader an unhappy person unable to overcome the pangs of jealousy.

Darwin noted that jealousy frequently took the form of rage, expressing itself in facial discolouration and heavy breathing, accompanied as often as not by verbal accusations. Look at the face of someone you know or suspect to be jealous. The facial expression is likely to bear the appearance of being 'eaten up' or gnawed or consumed by jealousy, a look or expression most apparent when someone discovers that a partner is having a sexual liaison with someone else. The person appears strained and anguished, and friends might say to each other how their friend 'has aged' or 'looks haggard'.

Common jealous reactions include angry, flashing eyes; contorted expressions of self-control which are sometimes described as 'a dark brow'; sidelong glances to check up on the partner who is with someone else; or, simply, resentful, bilious, 'black' looks cast in the direction of the person who gives occasion, rightly or wrongly, for jealousy.

Embarrassment is another common feeling people may wish to hide. It does not always manifest itself in blushing, but the face is a total giveaway if you know what the signals are.

An embarrassed Chinese or Japanese sucks air in quickly and audibly through the lips and teeth. For instance, if they are asked to do something which they know they cannot accomplish they will show their embarrassment in this manner.

Many Asian races will wave their hands back and forth in front of their face, the palms open outwards, to signal embarrassment or humility. Many Africans, Koreans, Filipinos, Chinese and Japanese laugh or giggle to express discomfiture, surprise and malaise.

Darwin observed that an embarrassed person looks down, an action sometimes known as lowering the eyes. Those who could be described as painfully shy or extremely self-conscious spend much of their time with lowered eyes, for their inability to hold your gaze without blinking, flinching, or looking away first is a well-known sign of embarrassment.

No one likes being stared at. It can be embarrassing. Experiments conducted in America showed that when motorists were stared at while waiting at red traffic lights, most of them accelerated away more quickly when the lights changed.

Social gatherings of all types are likely to include guests and participants who would wish the event to end as quickly as possible. If you fear being at an event and surrounded by people who ignore you, and you lack the social skills to get acquainted with total strangers, why not learn to spot or identify shy or embarrassed people like yourself?

Here are some pointers to finding your soulmate or a friendly face in a crowd. Self-conscious people are aware of their faces, so they spend more time fidgeting with their hair, or beard-tugging, moustache-twiddling, and playing or toying with their ear lobes or earrings.

Others smoke nervously, often flicking off bits of cigarette ash that have not really had time to form. Others sip their drinks nervously and frequently, while some gulp them down. Many snatch at every passing sandwich or canapé, consuming them without apparent enjoyment; others wipe their mouths so often on a napkin or handkerchief that you could be forgiven for thinking they had just consumed a meal of banquet proportions. What you are witnessing, though, are a variety of nervous actions that involve the face, performed to cover up feelings of social embarrassment and inadequacy.

The clumsy, ill-at-ease party-goers might also be seen with their heads and faces kept down and low, giving the impression of not wanting to be noticed. Tall people, self-conscious of their height, are inclined to do this, too. With their faces held uncomfortably low their eyes must swivel up in order to meet the gaze of other people.

Shy people often bite their bottom lips, or laugh nervously at quite the 'wrong' or inappropriate time. They say things they did not mean to say, and may then even compound their embarrassment by introducing the agonising question: 'Why did I say that?'

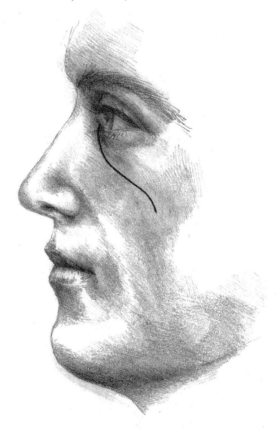

cheek line

A commonly observed facial line, or crease, is one which radiates from the inner corner of the eye (by the nose) and runs across and down the cheek. This line has two meanings. Firstly, it signifies the self-consciousness of someone who is likely to be best described as a fish out of water in most public or social situations. Secondly, the owner of such a crease is easily used, and taken advantage of, by others to further their ambitions.

In your search to identify the awkward and embarrassed among your friends, do not omit to include all those who make a habit of looking quickly away if they see something they feel they cannot cope with; for instance, the sight of a physically handicapped child, or a desire to avoid being caught looking at a famous person or celebrity – and especially not to be seen looking by the person who is the centre of attention.

If their eyes do inadvertently meet, the embarrassed man or woman will probably flash a quick apologetic smile, which could be interpreted as meaning, 'I'm sorry, I didn't mean to look at you'.

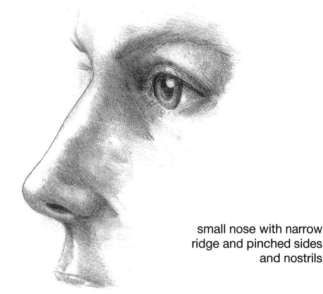

small nose with narrow
ridge and pinched sides
and nostrils

Men and women with a small nose with pinched sides, a narrow central ridge, and 'closed' or pinched nostrils are inclined to be anxious, timid, weak, self-effacing, and always at the ready to retreat into their shell rather than face up to conflict and the need for problem-solving.

Others likely to belong to the ranks of the faint-hearted are those with receding chins (see illustration on page 128). They need a companion, mate or guide whom they can trust and respect; without this support, they tend to be moody, irritable and stubborn.

receding chin

A *lack of confidence* is evident if a person has a tendency to blink very rapidly or swallow words in a conversation so that others have to strain to hear anything.

Facial features can be easily studied if you wish to discover who among your friends and colleagues lacks confidence or generally feels inferior. The facial features to look for are:

- flat or snub nose rising at an angle of less than thirty degrees at the point where the ridge rises from the bridge.
- jagged hairline.
- acute V-shaped hairline.

V-hairline

- red lines in the whites of the eyes. These lines also indicate a bad diet with fatty substances such as meat-fat predominating, or they can also warn of fatigue brought about by overworking.

More insecure than most, and the most likely to have an 'inferiority complex' are those who:

- only reveal their lower teeth when smiling.
- have tiny hollows or indents at the corners of the mouth.
- have eyes of different colours. Recognising the relevance of this, the French have a special adjective, *vairon*, to describe this condition.

When I lived and worked as a radio and television reporter in Paris, I took part in a programme about a tramp, or *clochard*, which won the Italia Prize.

The *clochard* was called Louis, and we followed him often for twenty-four hours at a stretch, recording the ways he filled his days searching for food, alcohol and a warm place to sleep.

When he begged, most people were too afraid to look him in the eye, even if they gave him money. I compared the faces of those who met his gaze with those who averted their eyes, and concluded that those who looked at his face tended to hold their heads upright and had wide-opened eyes, while those who avoided looking at him tilted their heads away from the tramp, often pursing their lips grimly as they hurried away. I also re-marked that the most generous donors not only met Louis' gaze, but also paused to talk with him.

We called the programme *An Unimportant Man*. To most he was an unimportant person, but if they had looked at his face and searched for the man behind the battered façade they would have found that Louis had many talents; he had in fact worked as a carpenter until he began drinking heavily after the breakup of his marriage.

There are certain facial signs that identify the men and women we tend to under-value and under-rate; among the most common traits are very small ears, particularly if they are thin and pressed flat against the side of the head.

Others to suffer from often inaccurate and arrogantly erroneous assumptions that they are weak and therefore of no consequence are the men and women whose faces are diamond-shaped: narrow at the fore-head and the chin (a pointed chin as a rule), and bulging cheekbones to give the diamond its widest point (see illustration on page 130).

Also likely to be under-rated are those with lips that meet to form a small, wavy line when the mouth is in repose (see page 28) and those with generously large mouths who do not mind speaking out and expressing their opinions. This latter facial quality belongs to many under-valued

diamond face

people, whose vibrant energy and outspoken enthusiasm for a rich variety of matters overwhelms and baffles the more restrained types. Above all, the narrow-minded feel instantly threatened by gregarious, outspoken people.

THE FOUR S'S

A clever face reader can look at the face of total strangers and know their four S's secrets: is this man or women *sensitive*, (over-sensitive or hyper-sensitive), *self-aware* (in touch with what makes him or her tick), *self-contained* (does not need anyone else most of the time), or *solo* (in-dependent and does not need anyone else)?

How can you look at the face of someone and say, 'This person is sensitive'?

When *sensitive* (creative and artistic) people take part in a conversa-tion they raise their eyebrows more frequently than the average man or woman. At the same time as the eyebrow is moving upwards, horizontal creases appear in mid-forehead. Their eyebrows are supple, pliant and flexible. And although the eyebrows can be thick or thin, arched or straight, the important thing to look for is their flexibility, when their owner reacts expressively to people, events and situations.

Anyone whose irises are surrounded by three areas of white instead of the usual two (in this instance the three areas are sited below and on each side of the iris of each eye) is sensitive and alert to what is going on around them (see page 120).

More than most, sensitive people flare or dilate their nostrils while they are talking or listening intently. As might be expected, the nostrils come into play when discriminating taste buds and an acute sense of smell are activated; for instance, if a sensitive person sniffs delicious scents from a perfume bottle or a chef's kitchen. Furthermore, the nostrils will flare when an aesthetic man or woman is sexually aroused.

We are usually baffled, maybe offended or hurt, if a person to whom we have given a gift, a compliment, our attention, or our time and goodwill shows no appreciation whatsoever. Our explanation is most likely that the recipient is ungrateful and we vow not to bother to help again. Those with an M-hairline are especially sensitive in this way. They expect fair play and abiding by the simple rules of give and take.

M-hairline

If you help another, be prepared for a negative or hostile reaction. A sensitive person hates to appear incompetent, unsuccessful, or under an obligation to you or anyone else. It signifies loss of face, and loss of their freedom. Moreover, these feelings are exacerbated if the person feels unable to return the favour.

There is another point that needs to be considered. Fine facial skin or a pale complexion announces to the face watcher that the owner has a fragile and sensitive face that needs protecting against exposure to the sun and wind.

When you are looking for those who are 'thin-skinned' in the sense of being sensitive to criticism or easily upset and offended, look instead for frosty faces with dull, pasty complexions. It is these which belong to persons who take offence easily; they lack a sense of humour and never, or hardly ever, see the funny side of a situation or event.

We have already seen how joining eyebrows that meet without a break denote jealousy. By separating the mind (forehead) from perception (eyes) joining eyebrows mean that their owner is also over-sensitive, unforgiving and liable to bear grudges, and always on the lookout to repay mean acts suffered on earlier occasions.

Touchy and generally humourless are those with down-turned mouth corners. This is also indicative of a kill-joy with a regular chip on the shoulder.

Over-sensitive in a totally different way is the person whose face shape resembles an inverted isosceles triangle (a triangle with two equal sides), that is, a pointed chin and a forehead which is not only wide and deep, but is also the widest part of the face. For this person is suspicious by nature, will rarely relax enough to put his or her trust in another, and inevitably manages to choose the wrong partner for a long-term relationship.

inverted
isosceles
triangle face

Perhaps the clearest giveaway of touchiness is the presence of a tiny 'V' dip in the upper lip. This V-shape is visible only when the lips are joined and the mouth is closed, and it also indicates a very timid person, but one likely to be utterly creative and ultra-refined in love-making (see page 97).

Hyper-sensitive and accident-prone are those unfortunate few who have an area of white *above* the iris in addition to the normal two areas on either side of the iris.

This brings us to the other side of the coin: the totally *insensitive*, inflexible, uncompromising person.

These people have passive faces, with little or no expression. There you will not find any interaction and there will be no mimicking. If you told them, for example, that you had just won a lottery, do not expect to see a flicker of joy on their face. They are out of tune with social situations and the feelings of others.

Self-aware and in touch with their emotions are those with small, thin ear lobes. These people are also fairly impractical though. Even mending a basically simple appliance will generally be beyond their capabilities.

If you can picture the ear divided into three zones, parallel zones each of about the same width, then consider first the top zone or upper part of the ear. If it is wider than either the middle or low zone, this reveals a fine mind coupled with sensitivity and loads of self-knowledge (see page 37 for the three zones of the ear).

Anyone with a very thin and angular jaw is not, as a rule, an amusing companion, but this man and woman will be fully aware of their worth to others. They are reflective and more likely to look before they leap than to be pushed into acting in the belief that time waits for no man.

Individuals who are preoccupied with their own inner feelings may often be seen 'deep in thought', with a faraway gaze which, temporarily at least, 'sees' nothing. Those who are aware of their own shortcomings will scan the faces of others with a steady, prying gaze to extract another's ideas, information and thoughts. This latter penetrating gaze ought not to be off-putting; on the contrary this deep gaze is friendly, interested, and enquiring. And well-meaning, too.

People who are *self-contained* do not seem to need many friends. They like to get away from everyday humdrum and the hustle and bustle of office life, family obligations, and dreary, menial chores. They tend to be serious and reliable, and, not being ready instigators of conversation they are likely to be irritated by small talk, time-wasting gossip, or shallow topics of conversation.

Seeming remote or distant to their more garrulous colleagues or family members, the self-contained man or woman can be identified by two very fascinating facial features.

The first is a small mouth. The second is a small, undeveloped tragus, the little knob or bump at the entrance of the earhole (see page 116). A small tragus is not visible if you look at a person's face from full on.

A third but less reliable indicator of those needing fewer friends or contacts than most is that the widest part of the face is formed by the cheekbones. This type of face is associated with slightly chilly, standoffish people, whose competence and apparent self-confidence arouse envy and quite often unjustified criticism.

And, finally, we have the most private, or laid-back people of all, for whom solitude, *solo*, 'doing it my way' or 'I want to be alone' are completely meaningful ways of going about their business or regulating their lives.

There is nothing outrageous about this. Most of us will sooner or later pretend not to see someone by looking the other way or appearing to be deep in thought and therefore distracted from friendly behaviour. Another sign that a person wants to be left alone is a temporary, blank look from expressionless eyes, so to speak. We are all inclined to adopt such an expression when we feel our privacy is threatened by the crowds pressing against us in a peak-hour commuter train, or as we jostle for a taxi after the theatre turns out on a wet night.

Another common facial gesture is to raise a barrier around the face and head with our hands in a restaurant, café, public library, bus, or cinema, for example, to signal to others, 'Private', 'Keep out', 'This is my space', 'Don't cramp me'.

The most private of individuals are likely to wear dark glasses at all times of the day and night, and many will have sunken, deep-set eyes. A considerable number have the archetypal Greta Garbo nose, one which is high, with a narrow, prominent ridge (running down the length of the nose), and with thin nostrils. Thin nostrils also warn of loneliness in middle and the third age.

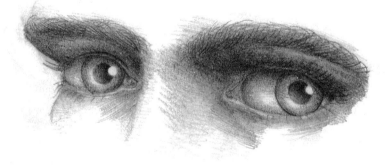

deep-set eyes

Another physical sign of the solo man or woman is a very flat area located between the side of the nose and the cheekbone.

All of these self-contained men and women value peace at all costs, and they are perfectly happy to be alone. You should be wary of marrying or hoping for a permanent relationship with the solo type. Be warned that you will have to work hard for this relationship to prosper.

Another relationship that requires more giving than taking in order to make it succeed is one with a man or woman with three special eye combinations: narrow, slanting up, and a hint of a squint. This trio of traits suggests to the expert face watcher that the owner is a loner, unable or unwilling to communicate their secret emotions to another.

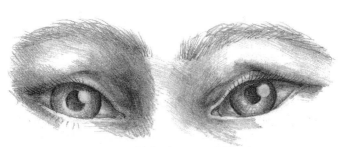

narrow eyes which slope up; hint of a squint

Life with anyone whose face is extremely bony and angular, with prominent cheekbones, jaw and nose will also be tough, for a lean, mean face is associated with militancy, spite and turbulence.

angular, bony face

Possibly the best kept secret of all is *loneliness*, for even if we are lonely few of us would like to admit it. On the whole loneliness derives from not having enough intimate conversations with friends or people we think understand us. Or, we experience loneliness if we feel awkward in a social group; we can be surrounded by a hundred or hundreds of people in a crowded room and still feel lonely.

Lonely people can sometimes be identified by their faces. Extremely thin nostrils, thin lips, or a weak gaze are all facial clues to a lonely person. Couple any one of these face signs with knowledge that this person is taking a lot of tranquillisers, or staying in most of the day watching television, or has ceased to talk about himself or herself to friends, and you have the picture of a lonely person. If you require more evidence of loneliness, look for impatience, boredom, and self-deprecation and you might think it is time to help.

Finally, look into the eyes to check up on loneliness. A lonely person often has a far-away or a soft look, and there is a flicker of hope that maybe you will say or do the right thing to bring this person back into the mainstream of events, without requiring a reward for your concern and efforts.

CHAPTER 10

BEAUTY AND THE BEAST

There is no single ideal of beauty. If there were, we would all yearn for the same face. Nonetheless, there are fashions and changing conventions about what constitutes beauty and good looks.

In ages past, perfect proportion was all the rage. For the ancient Greeks, the perfect face consisted of ideal thirds: the forehead would be one-third of the way down from the hairline, and the mouth one-third up from the lowest point of the chin. Moreover, the width of the face would equal two-thirds of its length.

In medieval Europe the perfect number was seven: at the top the hair spread over the upper seventh; the forehead occupied the next two-sevenths; the nose ran down the next two-sevenths; one-seventh was taken up by the space between the base of the nose and the mouth; and, the final seventh comprised the area below the mouth.

Even more fascinating, though, is a facial concept invented by an anonymous physician in Tunisia in 1180. In his book, *An Intelligent Man's Guide*, the scholar noted that men are attracted to certain parts of a woman's face, which are grouped in the lucky numbers of twos and threes. This is the list of 'Two Female Things' and 'Three Female Things':

three white things	complexion, whites of eyes, teeth
three red things	tongue, lips, cheeks
two round things	face, eyes
two long things	hair, eyebrows
two broad things	forehead, eyes
two narrow things	nostrils, ears
two small things	mouth, nose
two nice-smelling things	nose, mouth

Today's ideal face for Western tastes puts an oval shape at the top of the list for both men and women. Square-shaped faces are deemed attractive only in men (see page 43).

A smooth forehead is preferred for both male and female faces and there is general agreement that the forehead should be longer than the low zone (from nose tip to the chin).

Europeans prefer women's eyes to be large, bright, clear, soft, widely spaced and with long lashes, while American men responded to researchers' questions by expressing a liking for large and preferably blue eyes in their ideal woman.

Roman noses are thought desirable in men only, while small, slim noses are believed beautiful in women, particularly if the nose is also straight, and diamond-shaped, when seen from the front.

Europeans are rather attracted to men with stubbly skins, but prefer clear, pale, smooth skin for women. On the other side of the Atlantic too the preference is for clear skin for females, but a girlish freckled face also finds admirers.

There is general agreement that the ideal female mouth is small to medium sized, with gentle lips that are neither thick nor narrow. European women do not object to a large, strong mouth in their menfolk. However, there is a variation in the case of ears. The European ideal is for a female ear to be small, while North Americans speak of two 'must nots' for both male and female ears: the ears must not protrude and they must not have small lobes.

There is widespread agreement that female eyebrows are best if they are fine and gently arched, while men are all the better for having bushy eyebrows, wide chins and firm jaws. In Europe, a certain amount of facial hair contributes to a man's masculine appeal, but 'clean shaven' goes down better in America.

Physical differences between the sexes occur in the face as well as in other bodily parts. The female skin is generally finer, clearer and smoother, which makes those skin qualities desirable feminine attributes.

Furthermore, the female face is, on average, only about four-fifths the size of the male's. If it is larger or expressively mobile it is likely to be criticised for being too masculine. Many people feel threatened by an exuberant female face.

Female eyes are bigger, with the surrounding skin more susceptible to colour changes in health and blood circulation, giving the appearance of shaded tone, an effect which can be taken further by skilful cosmetic techniques.

Women's eyelashes are often longer than those of men, although their eyebrows tend to be thinner, finer and shorter than male brows. In addition, men usually have more prominent foreheads, but the exception here concerns intelligence and cerebral gifts. A 'brainy' woman will have a correspondingly brainy forehead: wide, rounded and smooth.

The female nose is smaller than its male counterpart, and it is also proportionately smaller in relation to the rest of the facial features. Women's noses are also more concave and their bridges flatter. The female mouth is relatively smaller, too, and the upper lip is likely to be shorter.

On the whole, the female chin and jaw are less pronounced than those of men, but a woman with a powerfully protruding chin will get most things in life which she sets out to achieve or acquire.

Winners of female beauty contests very often have facial features which are normally associated with cute children: large and widely spaced eyes (with large pupils), a relatively small nose area, a pretty mouth, and a small chin.

'Baby-faced' men and women are linked in people's minds with positive qualities and innocence, so much so that they are, in many legal systems, less likely than others to be thought guilty of committing a crime. Research in several countries has shown that acquittal rates favour the baby-faced. It is known, too, that adults are more lenient to a badly behaved, but good-looking, child than to an unattractive one.

baby-faced adult

Additional features associated with good-looking female faces are wide cheekbones and narrow cheeks, a straight nose with a fine, narrow tip, high-set eyebrows (far from the eyes), and a large smile displaying white, evenly shaped teeth.

There is a positive effect that beautiful women have on those who see them. Because of their 'halo effect' – the aura of their personal beauty – attractive women are attributed with having fewer medical problems than most, and are considered bright, sociable, and assertive.

There are more rub-off effects from good looks than meet the eye. If a physically unattractive man is seen in the company of a good-looking woman, he is adjudged professionally successful, is expected to be a high-income earner, and is thought to have a high IQ. On the other hand, it would appear that a physically unattractive woman gains little by being seen with a good-looking man. The chances are more that unenlightened tongues will wag and questions be asked.

'What does he see in her?' or 'He must be after her money' are commonplace remarks in such circumstances.

There is one final blow to anyone outside the category of the beautiful people: studies have shown that a person with a highly attractive face and demeanour is more likely to be recommended for a job than a plain-faced male or female applicant.

There is some consolation, though, for all of us whose faces would get nowhere in a Miss World or Mr Universe contest. However unconventional or bizarre one's appearance, it is safe to suppose that somewhere someone will love it.

In parts of Uganda and Sudan, for example, there are tribes who consider it appealing to have six front teeth missing. On the Pacific Islands of Trobriand and Yap, black teeth are thought particularly beautiful.

Enlarged, fat lips are a point of beauty in the area of Lake Chad (by the Nigeria-Niger border), and extremely flat, broad noses are reckoned to be desirable by the Cantonese.

Even being cross-eyed found favour among the Mayans of Central America, and to tell someone they are fat-faced would be a compliment among the Trarsa of the western Sahara and the Makololo of the Zambesi River, in Zambia.

MIRROR, MIRROR ON THE WALL . . .

There is more than a hint of dislike of women in the poet John Keats' address to

> Woman! when I behold thee flippant, vain,
> Inconstant, childish, proud, and full of fancies.

Yet, not all the world's vanity resides in women. Men try to hide a bald patch by combing an outsize long lock of hair over the telltale area, little suspecting how foolish they look when a gust of wind displaces the carefully arranged strands to reveal the bald bit.

hair-raising vanity:
before and after

Moreover, probably more often than women, men will stop in front of a mirror or shop window to comb their hair. In contrast, women who put on make-up or comb their hair in public places do so by gazing into a small mirror which is usually extracted from a handbag.

A few decades ago it was not uncommon to hear Dorothy Parker's homely but hurtful warning that 'Men seldom make passes at girls who wear glasses'.

Today, spectacles are lucrative money-spinners for the famous names in the couture business, among them Christian Dior, Valentino, Yves Saint-Laurent, Ralph Lauren and a host of top designers, but the trend is still to invest in and grapple with, contact lenses.

It is not altogether a rare event to find some temporarily blind person bent over the pavement patting the ground for a lost contact lens.

Some people wear sunglasses on dark and stormy nights and other odd times. There could be any number of explanations but the most likely are to hide a black eye, to protect the eyes during an allergic attack or infection, or, simply as an attempt to hide one's identity from inquisitive, prying eyes. There is another reason: fashion and vanity, for nowadays some of those designer sunglasses are extremely attractive and face-flattering.

LET'S KISS AND MAKE UP

When lovers quarrel and make it up with a kiss they do not expect her lipstick to turn his face red. Today's lipsticks glow in the dark, they are swim-proof, and, as the advertisers claim, they meet the requirement of staying where they are put.

Cosmetics were used liberally by men and women in ancient Greek, Roman, Egyptian, Hindu, and Chinese eras to enhance the human face. Cleopatra painted her upper eyelids blue and the lower lids emerald green. Her eyebrows were traced in black kohl and her face and neck were whitened with white lead. The *Kama Sutra* instructed every woman how to use cosmetics skilfully as one of her additional skills in seduction. The suggested methods included colouring the teeth and highlighting the eyes to make them appear bigger and rounder and therefore more appealing.

Young ladies of 'good breeding' in medieval England were happy to shave the hair from their upper forehead, though modern taste might not agree. The remaining hair was sometimes dyed bright sunflower yellow while the face was rendered deathly white by a covering of nasty white paste. In fact, some women died from the effects of the lead-based paints. Wiser women were content to stain their lips.

In the European courts at the same time the young women were putting rouge on their cheeks; some bathed and washed their faces in 'magic' liquids made from extraordinary blends of wolves' blood and crocodile glands.

Men like Beau Brummel led the way into the nineteenth century by setting new hygiene standards, cleaning their teeth, shaving, and pulling out hair growing from the wrong place on the face.

Today, the cosmetics industry spends billions of dollars, pounds, francs and marks to advertise their facial treatments for both sexes. Their customers part with many billions more, facing up to their failings and putting a brave face on things with the aid of the products they buy.

Coco Chanel, creator of the enduring Chanel No. 5 perfume, coaxed women to dab perfume in the places they wanted to be kissed. One such place, she suggested, was the ears. Another was the nose tip.

The future of perfumes for the end of the twentieth century is in the hands of the big French and American perfume houses. Predictions are for increasingly complex blends of cedarwood enhanced by plum, peach, cinnamon and vanilla. Some perfumes already go as far as including chocolate, caramel and coffee among their ingredients.

By the year 2000, then, it seems that men will be kissing faces that evoke the kitchen smells of homemade jams and fruit pies.

UPLIFTING FACES

Unless a face is made up by an absolute expert, an onlooker can nearly always tell if someone is wearing cosmetics. It is by no means as easy to tell whether they have had cosmetic surgery.

Cosmetic surgery was first practised in India more than a thousand years ago. The medieval church in Europe opposed the idea, which it described as interference with God's work. Many early practitioners were condemned as sorcerers.

Nowadays, people hail the miracles that can be achieved by plastic surgeons, particularly in repairing the deformities and disfigurements resulting from accidents and wars. No less remarkable are the achievements that surgeons have accomplished in correcting congenital deformities such as harelips, birthmarks and red 'port wine' stains.

The last ten years have seen a rapid rise in the numbers of people seeking the help of surgery to improve, or at least change, their facial appearance. Cosmetic surgery is most readily practised on the nose, chin, ears and eyes, but it can also change the contours of the face and affect the measurements of other facial features.

Rhinoplasty, the alteration of the nose, familiarly known as the 'nose job', is one of the most common operations. A large nose can be diminished by removing bone or cartilage. A flat nose can be given new shape by means of a carved implant. As the incisions are made inside the nasal cavity no scars are visible and it is difficult for those who were not familiar with the person's face before to tell whether or not the nose has been surgically altered.

Prominent ears – which, contrary to popular belief, have nothing to do with babies being permitted to sleep on a folded-over ear – can easily be made to lie flat nowadays by simple surgery. This operation is a particular boon to men who are self-conscious about having 'jug handle' ears, who otherwise could only hide their obtrusive ears by growing their hair long as women would do.

Alterations to correct receding chins or change the size or shape of the mouth are also now quite routine work for plastic surgeons. Moreover, eyebrows can be raised, bags removed from under the eyes, worry creases eradicated from furrowed brows, double chins reduced, and oriental 'single' eyelids can be changed to a Western 'double' lid.

If the customer requires a total facelift the surgeon can accomplish that by separating the facial skin and some of the skin of the neck by means of an incision just beyond the hairline. Then the skin is pulled up towards the temples and back towards the ears to tighten it. Those perpetually in search of rejuvenation might return several times over the years to have the surgical procedures repeated.

How is the face reader to cope with this surgical interference with the evidence? Is it in fact possible to make an accurate reading of a face which has undergone repair work or surgical transformation?

The first thing is to understand that no corrective, remedial or beautifying changes achieved by cosmetic surgery can alter a person's basic character. The only effects that it can bring about are a certain amount of extra happiness, a degree of extra confidence, and an enhanced feeling of self-esteem derived from the belief that one's looks have been improved.

Next, bear in mind that the majority of people who have cosmetic surgery do not have a total face change. The exceptions are those who have been in a particularly bad accident or are victims of a horrible disaster such as a fire. In cases where an entirely new face has been artificially created, the face reader cannot form proper conclusions about the person's character from the facial features, which probably bear no resemblance to the individual's original, or natural, appearance.

Countering any inaccuracy in cases where only a single feature has been altered, though, should not be too difficult. The important point to remember here is that when studying a person's face to assess their character one should always look at the *whole* face, its shape, structure, expressions and gestures, and not rely on a reading of a single feature to the exclusion of all others.

If, for example, you assess a person's nose for such characteristics as power, creativity, strength, and a host of traits and personal tendencies which the nose reveals (these are featured in the relevant chapters, and can be identified by means of the index), you may then notice something anomalous, and suspect a 'nose job'. Your findings and suspicions should be checked by looking at other parts of the face, which will confirm or deny your original analysis.

Millions of men and women rejoice in their new-look noses, chins, or indeed, their wholly renovated faces. But there are also some unsuccessful efforts. Occasionally some operations end in rather grotesque facial distortions, though in those cases the fact that they are the result of unskilful surgery means they are likely to be quite easily detected.

Generally, it is features that appear too good to be true that should be most suspected. For example, those who have a retroussé nose, which turns up slightly at the tip, are not normally energetic or pushy, but a retroussé nose (sometimes referred to as a 'pug' or 'button' nose) is generally considered a particularly cute attribute on a female face. It is a safe bet that no woman would want to cut off a retroussé nose by substituting for it any other model.

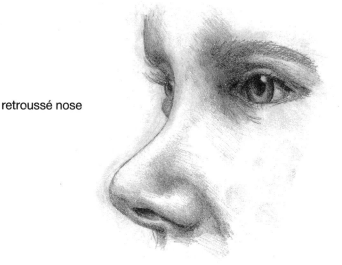

retroussé nose

On the other hand look carefully at pushy, ambitious and energetic women who have cute little button noses turning up prettily at the tip. It is quite possible that little organ of smell and respiration is not the one they were born with.

People's reasons for submitting to the cosmetic surgeon's knife are many. For some there is the hope that their marriage will benefit from an extension of their apparent youthfulness, but if that is the case then the relationship is really going to require something more than cosmetic surgery to make it worthwhile. Our prospects for happiness are enhanced if we can face up to the future realistically, and act according to our age.

GROWING OLDER ALL THE TIME

Few of us realise that the only part of the face which retains its shape from birth to death is the ear. Although the ear will grow, it will retain its proportions and features for the owner's lifetime. Otherwise, at every age some part of the face swells, retracts, sags, softens or changes outline. The baby-faced forehead no longer juts out, baby fat drains away from the cheeks, noses lose their deep concave scoop, chins advance (or not), jaws grow more angular, and . . . the ears do tilt backwards.

By observing his own children Charles Darwin discovered the age at which infants and small children could kiss, smile to show affection, smile to express amusement or laugh to mean 'I'm amused.' Describing his infant's pain on one occasion he noted that the mouth curved into an exaggerated horseshoe and the 'expression of misery then becomes a ludicrous caricature.'

At another time Darwin described creases that formed on his child's forehead during a bout of prolonged crying. 'The forehead develops vertical, central and transverse functions resembling a triangle,' but he found them less marked in children than in an adult's face because young skin does not wrinkle. Like many of his generation Darwin believed that human facial expressions are innate rather than learnt, and the argument persists today and probably forever, as to whether our facial reactions and expressions are with us at birth or whether they are acquired from experience of life itself.

Another argument concerns family resemblances: some researchers believe genetic similarities of facial features are really based on family *codes of expression*, but others support the idea that if we have the same nose shape as, for example, our father, the resemblance is *structural* rather than one based on expression.

As a man ages so his eyebrows usually grow thicker, longer and coarser. On the other hand, a woman's eyebrows and eyelashes thin out as she ages. In both sexes, the hairs will fall out if kidney or bladder problems occur.

In the ageing process the eyes gradually deteriorate. After the age of about ten the best viewing distance lengthens gradually until, by the age of fifty, many have to wear spectacles to correct this long-sightedness. Moreover, as we get older we have greater difficulty changing focus and recovering from the effects of glare. Add to this a poorer performance in visual acuity, matching of colours, and seeing in the dark.

With age, our blink reflex gets slower, the eyelids hang loosely because of poorer muscle tone, and there is an increased likelihood of dizziness. With great age, the eyes appear sunken owing to a gradual loss of orbital fat.

Although the outward appearance of the ears remains stable there is plenty going on inside to mark the passage of time. First, there is a gradual loss of hearing, and very high tones are lost completely. Many with failing hearing ability will gaze intently at the speaker's mouth in an involuntary attempt to lip-read.

The mouth changes dramatically with age. The gums recede, less saliva is secreted, and both senses of smell and taste become less acute. There is reduced sensitivity to salt and sugar, and there are problems of chewing because the facial muscles become weaker and some teeth will be lost.

Movements of the lips change with age, too. Speech becomes slower, pauses longer and more frequent. Breathing is heavier and more rapid after exertion, such as running to catch a bus, carrying heavy shopping, or climbing stairs. The voice loses power, often becoming higher-pitched or even piping and brittle. Slurring is not uncommon in the elderly and senile.

As we grow old the skin loses its bloom and elasticity, so it hangs in folds and wrinkles around the eyes, under the chin and around the corners of the mouth, and in the lower cheeks. Wounds such as bruises to the cheeks or cuts made when shaving take longer to heal, and the skin is likely to itch more.

The bleached look on facial skin is not uncommon in freckled red-heads as they age, and we are all likely to get brown stains or patches (age spots) on the forehead, cheeks, chin and lips, often coinciding with similar brown marks on the backs of the hands, as we grow older.

Our hair responds to the ageing process by thinning and greying. Some will resent their grey hairs, but others feel distinctly more distinguished.

The face reveals to face readers the lucky men and women most likely to retain their youthful looks well into their sixties and even eighties. The super-young often have plump cheeks, although they will be a little overweight. Their face will stay smoother and younger as they age than will a face with prominent or high cheekbones, and slim or hollow cheeks. This latter combination of cheeks and cheekbones is associated with a model's good looks or the lean look of some of the virile stars of Hollywood Westerns, but remember, these fine faces wear out and lose their physical beauty much more rapidly than those of puffy, plump-cheeked men and women, because haggardness and gauntness strike deftly when there is no fat to resist.

A retroussé nose – which is small, pert, and turns up – has a childish quality which makes its owner appear far younger than he or she really is. Full lips also help to give a face a youthful quality, especially as our lips tend to wither and collapse with age.

Dr David Weeks, a psychologist based in Edinburgh, believes it is easier to look young if you are affluent and have had a stable life. However, he stresses that too much sun and smoking, and even using the face a lot to express one's feelings are all bad if we wish to cheat the ageing process. Dr Weeks also believes that depressed people look older than their years, but that an exceptionally good sex life will contribute to a super-young image.

Anyone with low-placed ears (when the lobes or half the ear reach below the level of the nose) is generally a late developer, often doing best in the last third of his or her life. Those with a round face can also look considerably younger than they really are well into middle and old age.

There is a section given to centenarians in Chapter 8, but we may note here that in America researchers give hope to anyone who wants to live a very long time. There are, according to Dr Caleb Finch of the University of Southern California and Dr James Carey of the University of California at Davis, two basic models of ageing. The traditional theory is the 'time-bomb model' which supposes that, starting from a certain age, we 'self-destruct'.

The other theory, based on research done on a group of fruit flies, is the 'spaceship model', which likens our life span to that of a spaceship engineered to reach a particular goal, yet which may still prove capable of going a little further. Dr Carey's optimistic findings support the spaceship model, and suggest that there is no fixed age at which everyone must be dead.

The last word concerning this important subject of ageing must go to the fruit fly Methuselahs: some are now living twice as long as is normal for their species, which means that if humans can follow the success path of the fruit fly there are going to be a lot of us around in the year 2100 – and beyond. So let us not fly in the face of progress, but put on a brave face and face up to the future and the joys it might bring.

THEM AND US

One of the most common questions asked about face reading is what part racial differences play in making an accurate assessment of a person's character and personality.

To be a successful face watcher and judge of character it is necessary to know something about the facial shapes and proportions of the races you are likely to meet or wish to understand. Unless you live on a secluded island without ever seeing another living soul or outside the reach of radio or television signals, you will have ample opportunities to become familiar with the faces of the nations of the world.

It is well known, for instance, that the Japanese have narrower eyes than most people, and that the ears of the black races tend to be smaller than others.

Narrow eyes generally signal slyness and self-sufficiency. Small ears indicate a need to work hard if their owner wants to achieve anything worthwhile in life. Now, it is *not* possible that all Japanese are sly, or best left to their own devices. Nor can it be true that all black men and women have to work uniformly hard to get on.

What the face reader has to do, knowing these two racial traits, for instance, is to imagine or compare a group of five or six persons of the same race. Among a group of Japanese, for example, one person may have very narrow eyes, others moderately narrow eyes and some comparatively wide or big eyes. The experienced face reader will attribute the narrow eyes' characteristics of slyness and self-sufficiency *only* to the Japanese individual with eyes which are notably narrow, even for a person of that race.

Similarly, the smallness of black people's ears will vary, and the necessity to work hard to achieve goals in life will be in inverse relationship to the size of their ears.

As a guide to some of the principal facial differences between races, here is a short summary of carefully researched observations: Blacks and Europeans tend to have long heads, while Chinese have relatively broad heads and faces.

The racial differences are pronounced in the size and shape of our teeth. For example, the Japanese tend to have smaller mouths than most and relatively thick teeth. Many of them also have four roots to a molar instead of the more common two or three. Indians, Pakistanis, Bangladeshis, Iraqis, and Iranians have something in common: smaller teeth (in height and width) with fewer spaces between them.

Chinese have quite large teeth (in total surface area), while many Africans have even larger teeth with long roots. South of the Sahara, Africans very often have a big gap between the top incisors, and teeth and jaws make up a bigger proportion of the face than is usual among most other races.

Europeans generally have smaller, squarer teeth, while many members of the Amazonian tribes have unusual triangular-shaped top front teeth, each tooth coming to a sharp point at the cutting edge. In addition, many tribesmen and women of the Amazon region lack pre-molars.

Caucasian noses are narrow compared to most negroid noses, and Caucasians often have a high bridge and a long nose tip; negroid noses are generally broad, with a wide, flat bridge, and a thick tip.

In between these nose varieties are the Mongoloids of Central Asia and other Asian race groups. Their noses are usually more concave and set flatter in the face. The bridge is modestly narrow and flat. Southern Chinese tend to have plump nose tips and quite broad nostril wings, too.

Many findings concerning the nose were proposed by the remarkable Mikhail Gerasimov, the Russian scientist who perfected the reconstruction of the human face from a skull. Professor Gerasimov's most famous subject was Tamerlane, who conquered Central Asia and parts of India and died on his way to an invasion of China. Gerasimov was able to put a face to the skull of the conqueror. Others to have received the Gerasimov treatment were the German poet Schiller and the Russian Tsar Ivan the Terrible.

Tamerlane's face was reconstructed with a thick beard, curly eyebrow hairs, and hair growing to a length of three centimetres on the temples.

Chinese and Japanese hair is inclined to be straight and smooth; curly hair is common in Western Europe, Australia, New Zealand and North America; woolly and sometimes frizzy hair is commonly found in Africa.

The colour of the eyes has also been examined in connection with race. As a general rule, pale eyes go with pale hair and dark eyes with darkish hair, but as with all observations about race there are exceptions.

The mouth shows considerable variations. Full and wide, thick lips are found among most black races, in contrast to the thinner and paler lips of Europeans.

There is a tendency to make sweeping generalisations about temperamental differences between the races. For instance, dark-haired Latins are associated with vivacity, excitability and talkativeness, while the pale, long-faced North Europeans are believed to be quiet, calm and introverted. It has to be stressed that race and temperament are not in fact so simply related; some of us will have met talkative, noisy Swedes or placid, quiet Italians.

In 1959 UNESCO issued a *Statement on Race*. The report made it clear that there was no relationship between race and temperament, and that all types of temperament can be found in every race.

The UNESCO *Statement* declared: 'The scientific investigations of recent years fully support the dictum of Confucius: "Men's natures are alike; it is their habits that carry them far apart"'.

One could usefully add to this a sample of graffiti from New York's Bronx, that 'racial prejudice is a pigment of the imagination'. The truth of that sets the scene for queries such as, 'Are all Chinese inscrutable?' or 'Do all Japanese look the same?'

The answer to the Chinese question is that Chinese are no more inscrutable than people of other nationalities. If they want to hide their feelings or disguise their inner thoughts, people of all nationalities can appear inscrutable to others unskilled in detecting their secrets. But the art of face reading, like so much other human knowledge and discovery, was developed first among the Chinese who are just as fit subjects for face reading as anyone else.

The reply to the Japanese question is simply this: if you think every Japanese looks the same then you are not looking at their faces with sufficient interest. Admittedly it is more difficult to distinguish people when they all have dark brown eyes, black hair and black eyebrows, but to understand the person and character behind each face you must learn to read all the *details*, not just the superficial headlines. If you are interested in getting to know other people, you will quickly see the differences.

New York City's policemen and women are trained to 'read' the faces of people of ethnic minorities so that they can identify them more accurately and recognise their descriptions.

It is worth remembering, too, that to Chinese, Japanese, Thai or Korean eyes, there is little easily recognisable difference between the faces of the white nationalities of Europe, North America and Australasia.

Details of physical differences between male and female faces were given earlier in this chapter. There are also differences in the sexes' face reading skills.

Women are better at recognising faces, and superior at perceiving and interpreting facial clues. For example, women notice more quickly when a person is sad, or ill, or out of sorts, probably because they look and make eye contact with others more readily than would a man. Women are more competent at judging the emotional state of others by face reading and picking up non-verbal cues and clues.

Whether you are male or female, if you have difficulty recognising people you feel you know but whom you cannot put a name to, or remember where you met, then you are most probably one of the many poor face readers who look at the air around the head and face of another person instead of looking directly at the face itself.

The less information we have about someone, the more we revert to pigeon-holing them into gender stereotypes. For instance, we see a colleague's wife wheeling a trolley in a supermarket and conclude that she is a housewife. Maybe she is on this particular occasion, but she could also be a maths wizard.

Hairy bits

Hair growth on the face provides hair-raising tales, among them Johnny Carson's much quoted observation on his *The Tonight Show* that while hair and fingernails might continue to grow for three days after we die, people tend to phone or call us less. Face readers should know, though, that a heavy growth of hair in the ear, especially if it is disproportionate to the rest of the head and body, tells the world that its bearer dissipates his or her energy, and so runs quickly out of steam. Sometimes very talented people waste their ideas and gifts, if their ears are especially hairy.

There are six reasons for a man to grow and cultivate a beard. First, he may want to hide an unattractive or misshapen jaw. Second, he might want to conceal a double-chin gained from gluttony, heavy drinking or lassitude, all of which are generally accompanied by a fat belly.

Third, he may want to assume an 'artistic' or 'primitive' appearance, or wish to affect 'intellectual' inclinations. Or, maybe he wants or needs to hide blemishes. Perhaps he hates having to shave, or is lax and lazy about his appearance. There is another explanation: like scientists stationed at the Poles, many men grow beards to keep warm.

Men who grow thick beards or moustaches are able to turn their minds to a number of subjects. Multi-talented, they have problems deciding in which field or discipline their greatest gifts lie. Men who can only grow sparse beards or moustaches do not know their true worth. Unwilling to push their talents to the limit, often because they fear failure, many could achieve more in life by taking more chances instead of exercising caution.

A bald patch or several bald areas in the beard or moustache belong to a man who would have thrived in an earlier era, one which would have better suited his values, hopes and aspirations.

NOSTRILS

Nostril-watching is fun; see facing page. It is not the most comfortable way of reading a face, but a quick glance up a person's nose will give you a fair indication of what lies beyond those quaint, and sometimes beautifully structured, orifices: the nostrils.

WINKS AND SQUINTS

People do not wink when they are alone. If they do, it is a tic. Winks are public or collusive acknowledgment of a shared, and possibly a secret, experience.

Squints are rarely beautiful. A tendency is for the master eye to fix its gaze on a person or object while the other eye is angled in a slightly

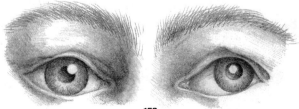

Nostril-watching

outgoing; adventurous; likes
having fun

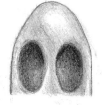

self-satisfied; weak-willed;
conservative

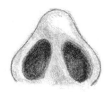

envious, but loath to admit
it; sense of humour

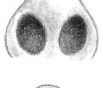

innovative; likes a challenge

excitable; may be
voluptuous; intuitive

attention-getter; liable to
bear grudges

insensitive; thick-skinned

different direction. A considerable amount of research into squint and its implications for face reading has been done in France. The conclusions are that different directions of squinting have different meanings:

- left eye upwards — over-sensitive; very sentimental
- right eye upwards — extremely intellectual
- left eye outwards — questioning, thoughtful, easily depressed
- right eye outwards — instinctive, capricious
- left eye inwards — fearful, narrow-minded
- right eye inwards — spiteful, quarrelsome
- left eye up and out — irrational, day-dreamer
- right eye up and out — lacks discipline and self-control

EYELASHES

Eyelashes reveal a variety of traits to a face watcher:

- long, straight — virile feelings; strength
- short, straight — moderate energy; tires easily
- long, curved — sensual, feminine traits, pliant; understands the under-dog, but often lacks generosity
- short, curved — limited energy; easily scared if confronted with an unknown, unfamiliar situation; faint-hearted

MOLES

A mole may be large or small, flat or raised, or smooth, warty, or with hair growing from it. The most highly prized mole is popularly called the 'beauty spot', the favourite places for which are on the highest point of the cheekbone or just above one corner of the mouth.

Many women use ink or pencil to create a beauty spot to draw attention to their face. This was a common practice among Hollywood film stars in the Fifties and Sixties, and before that, in the era of silent films.

A number of facial moles reveal some important facts about their possessor's character and personality.

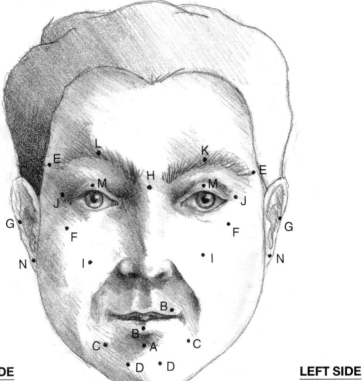

RIGHT SIDE   **LEFT SIDE**

A   Serious thinker at an early age.

B   Digestive disorders, especially after age fifty. The mole or moles may occur anywhere on the lips or near the upper lip.

C   Decisive.

D   Aggressive, stern.

E   Pensive; melancholic. The mole or moles may appear anywhere between the ends of the eyebrows and hairline.

F   The *natural* beauty spot, which indicates a lack of authority.

G   Ambition exceeds ability.

H   Immense sexual desire. This mole may occur anywhere on the bridge of the nose.

I   Attracted more by intellectual matters than material benefits. This mole is near mid-cheek.

J   Honest, straightforward. This mole is found at the outer corner of the eyes.

K   Lazy and selfish. The mole or moles are found among the hairs of the left eyebrow.

L   Great determination; a fighter. This mole is on the right eyebrow.

M   Talented, but under-valued by friends, employers, colleagues. This applies to a mole, or moles, situated on the eyelids.

N   Unreliable friend; uses others to get on. This is a misshapen (long) mole found on the ear lobe.

All Creased Up

Tamerlane the Mongol conqueror shows his face again. In the section concerning cosmetic surgery, we saw how the Russian scientist, Mikhail Gerasimov, reconstructed the warrior's face. In his celebrated tragedy, *Tamburlaine the Great*, the English dramatist Christopher Marlowe wrote '. . . in a mirror we perceive the highest reaches of a human wit'.

The mirror also reveals our creases, which comprise not only the tell-tale signs of ageing but also the character lines that reveal something about the mind.

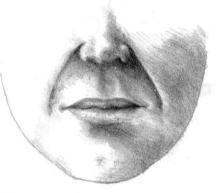

The lines end at mouth-level. If this person is sufficiently motivated he or she can make a success of any project.

The lines extend into the chin. Success arouses envy or jealousy, which acts as a brake on this person's contentment.

This person has the unusual ability to combine an understanding of business practices with artistic work. If the chin is strong (square or smoothly rounded and protruding) and if he or she has a powerful gaze, this person has top leadership potential.

156

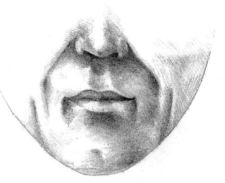

This man or woman would make a competent president, premier or head of a nation.

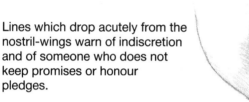

Lines which drop acutely from the nostril-wings warn of indiscretion and of someone who does not keep promises or honour pledges.

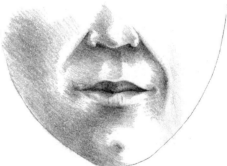

Lines of different lengths signal a lack of stamina and strength when willpower is needed.

Lines set on divergent paths indicate instability.

157

It is important to take into account the length and depth of a line or crease when you read a person's facial creases. If the line you are examining is short, fine, irregular, or broken, the quality or defect that it signals is diminished and reduced.

A total absence of lines on the face of a man or woman aged forty or more could indicate that this person has had cosmetic surgery. However, this observation is more likely to be true of a European face; Asian faces, in particular Chinese, Thai, Japanese and Korean, tend to crease much later than faces of the Western variety.

The only way to keep lines, creases and wrinkles at bay longer than normal according to the Chinese and the nomadic tribes and groups of the Arabian, Central Asian and African deserts, is to cover your face with a veil. This advice is particularly apposite for anyone spending the day in bright light or sunshine. If this sounds too troublesome, the alternative is to grow creases and wrinkles that will be yours for life!

THE BEAST

We all have our nasty side. There is a bit of the beast in all of us. There are ways and means of telling how beastly people can be by reading their faces.

Repulsive behaviour often involves parts of the face. People who fidget with their ears or noses, pick their teeth in public, or comb their hair over food are plainly being inconsiderate of others' feelings and sensitivities, but many people succumb to such social lapses once in a while.

The widespread, though wholly deplorable, habit that drivers have of picking their noses when their vehicle is stopped at traffic lights, for example, is explained, if not excused, by a tendency to regard their car or van as a private space, like their bedroom or bathroom. They are oblivious of the fact that everybody can see right into it.

How deep anti-social and unpleasant character traits go can be told by looking at the facial features themselves, and not, luckily, by making a study of the visually repulsive use their owners sometimes make of them.

Supposing stubbornness is the reason why the nose-picker clings to his or her unattractive habit, we can search the face for signs of this obdurateness. Stubborn people have no idea how adversely they affect other people. They defy logic, argument, common sense and pleas for the slightest bit of give and take. They make us angry, but they will not be moved. They put their faces down to avoid eye contact, or close their eyes.

Stubborn people who will cause the most irksome difficulties are those with the two top central incisor teeth disproportionately wider than the

two big,
central incisors

surrounding teeth. Individuals with this dental pattern have a problem admitting that they are in the wrong; they set their teeth against it.

There are many signs of obstinacy, among them:

● perfectly straight eyebrow tips (the end nearest the ear);

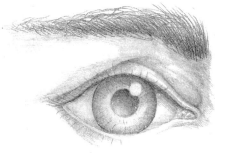

eyebrow with
straight tip

● only the lower row of teeth shows when the person smiles;
● a broad, receding chin and the jaw line drops almost vertically from below the ear (obstinacy is tempered if the jaw *curves* from below the ear to the chin); and
● when viewed full frontally, the broadest part of the nose is the middle portion.

The habit of taking others for granted is also very damaging to re-lationships. A deep rectangular-shaped face (that is, about the same width across the forehead, cheekbones and jaw, with straight sides) is associated with those who take advantage of others. Now look at the ear illustrated on page 160, for further indications of this unpleasant habit:

● a sharply angled corner or a sharp bend on the helix (outer rim) of the ear;
● a sharp bend on the inner circle (anti-helix) of the ear.

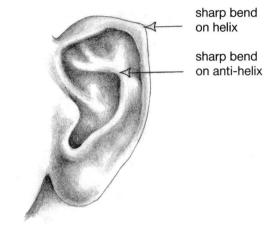

sharp bend
on helix

sharp bend
on anti-helix

Ungrateful people are inclined to be conceited. You can recognise the characteristics of conceit and narcissism in the face too: anyone with a cleft, dimple, or 'valley' in the centre of the chin craves and thrives on publicity.

Many people have this 'conceit cleft', among them George Bush, Larry 'J.R.' Hagman, Shimon Peres and Yitzhak Rabin of Israel, Yasser Arafat, Humphrey Bogart, and Kirk and Michael Douglas.

conceit cleft

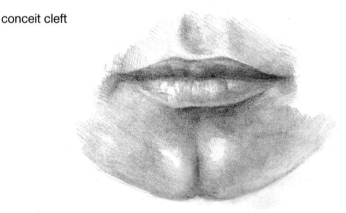

Many with a conceit cleft are hypocrites, suitably kitted out with 'two faces'. Being two-faced might be a virtue in politics or diplomacy or show-business, but it is a beastly trait in human relationships.

Another pointer to conceit or immense self-confidence is the ability to elevate the wing of one nostril at a time, a pertinent flare of the nostril to show the sniffer's disdain.

Snobs and social climbers are positively beastly at parties and social gatherings. For a while, say up to ten seconds, you might get their un-

one nostril
elevated to
express disdain

divided attention, but then they are looking over your head (if you are shorter) or to the left and right of your face in order to see if someone more important is within sight to move on to.

Snobs, with ideas above their station, conscious of class differences and intent on climbing the social ladder, are often endowed with sharp noses. A super-snob might well have a nose to compete with that of the Concorde.

Few of us thrive in the company of a supercilious man or woman. No one likes to be mocked for long. It is a universal trait for sarcastic or supercilious people to crinkle the nose as if they have just inhaled a bad smell. It

sneering with the
mouth and nose

permanently
sneering mouth

could be described as a sneer gesture, but whatever you call it, it is quite unattractive. As common as the sneer nose gesture is the permanently sneering mouth, where the lips are joined by an upward curving line, as seen when the mouth is in repose; in addition, the sneer mouth corners turn down.

A long, narrow tongue also tells the world that its owner is sarcastic, but we rarely catch sight of another person's tongue. That is a treat reserved mainly for doctors and dentists.

Evincing scorn, contempt or a 'stuck-up' notion of being somehow superior are not attractive attitudes or expressions, but they are sometimes adopted by people anxious to disguise their true feelings of inadequacy or inferiority.

Their face language is easy to read: they tilt their heads back, chin and nose stuck in the air, giving our language expressions such as 'she has her nose in the air' or 'being stuck-up'.

Contempt might involve looking down one's nose at, for example, someone's suggestion to see a film or buy a new CD. In these instances, we look down our noses at someone's efforts to please, while the nose in the air attitude is a gesture to avoid direct eye contact and so belittle the person we hold in contempt.

Contempt can be brutal. A hard, unfriendly stare without a hint of a smile is often reserved for those we deem inferior. Sometimes it can be a blatant display of hostility. Others show their dislike and contempt by raising their voices, even shouting at someone who cannot follow the language. You may have noticed this happening at police stations, railway booking offices, immigration entry points, anywhere in fact, where foreign visitors or migrants cannot understand what the official is saying to them.

Nasty

What is nasty to me may not be nasty to you, but most of us might settle for a short list of nasty traits which manifest themselves in facial expressions or, in certain cases, in the structure of the face.

The face reveals brutality by the following features:

- the lower lip overlaps the upper lip;
- a cold, hard gaze that sends shivers (of fear) down the spine; and
- very thick, bushy (and probably curly) eyebrows.

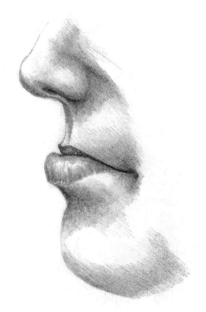

lower lip overlaps
upper lip

A cruel face shares some of the characteristics of the brutal face. In addition, these are further facial signs to be on one's guard against:

- aquiline nose that is hooked and curved like an eagle's beak. Unless they overcome their cruel instincts, should they live long, these people are doomed to a lonely old age;
- thin, dry, pale lips;
- eyebrows shaped like a boomerang (see page 62);
- a sneering, curled upper lip (like a snarling dog's); and
- thin lips, especially if they are crooked, twisted or do not meet (when the mouth is in repose).

Some people's faces are a catalogue of nasty character traits, but few of us are without any detracting features. For example, a person with a diamond-shaped face (widest at the cheekbones, but with a narrow forehead and a tapered or pointed chin) holds grudges and dwells on the hurts and ills inflicted by those they think wish them harm.

Additionally, anyone with a pointed chin which also veers to one side, that is, a crooked, pointed chin, is capable of bearing grudges for a lifetime.

There are further indicators which betray unforgiving men and women:

- a bumpy, uneven surface in the area between the eyebrows;
- scant hairs growing in this same area between the eyebrows; and
- a crooked mouth. This also signals dishonesty, unless it is the result of an accident or illness.

Spite and revenge can be detected by a skilful face reader. For example, many vengeful people have thin, crooked lips. But the person to be afraid of is one whose whole face is distorted. An irregular face might have a crooked mouth; a ragged, crooked jaw; one eye higher or much bigger than the other; ears of different size and shape; an off-centre, bumpy, swollen nose which attracts your instant attention by its presence; and a crooked smile. A face which includes three or more major irregularities such as these belongs to a person to be wary of at all times. However, it has to be stressed again that if this unhappy facial condition is the result of an accident or illness, the unfortunate owner cannot be blamed for an adverse face reading.

INSULTS

You do not need a vast, rich or colourful vocabulary to be able to hurl message-laden insults. As long as there is movement in your face you have a potent weapon.

To show their disrespect, people sneer or contort their face while thrusting it close to another's. They might turn the face away and pointedly ignore the other. Sighs and yawns (sometimes barely covered by the hand or sometimes mock yawns) or the glazed, far-away look adopted by those who feign scorn or disdain are familiar to most of us.

The ways in which parts of the face can be used to insult and humiliate are legion. The mouth, for example, can sneer cursorily (when one corner twitches up and out with a rapid movement before resuming its normal position). We blow a raspberry or spit in the direction of someone or we give a pinched, tight, chilly and contemptuous smile. Insults made by a silent but expressive face can be more telling than the most picturesque swear words in any language.

Another way intentionally to hurt a friend or colleague, for example, is to wink knowingly or conspiratorially at a third person so that the 'victim' sees you. Or, if you wish to convey to another that you think he or she is crazy, you might thumb the nose (put your thumb against your nose tip and fan out the fingers vertically in front of your face), or even more insulting, screw your index finger into the temple to imply, 'You are mad!'

These gestures are spiteful and malicious, but also temporary. Their occasional use does not mean that the people who employ them are essentially malevolent and malign. Always be on your guard, though, against any person with a projecting lower lip atop a protruding upper chin. They are uncompromisingly combative, confrontational and heartless.

protruding
lower lip

A further confirmation of nastiness and treachery is a crooked nose tapering to a very pointed tip. Owners of this nose are chronically and emotionally weak, and, when they feel threatened by events or people over whom they have no control or influence, they will strike out like a cornered cat.

crooked nose,
pointed tip

More treachery lies behind any pair of deep-set and extremely narrow eyes. If the eyes are more normal in size yet deep-set, this configuration suggests nothing more than secretiveness. You will find more about the secret-self in Chapter 9.

CRIMINALS

All the facial characteristics described as signs of nastiness, spite, malice, treachery, and malevolence in this chapter can be used as pointers to anti-social, even criminal types.

In the past 2000 years numerous face readers and face watchers have tried to identify the face of a criminal, but their efforts have largely amounted to guesses and unsubstantiated observations. They put on the list of suspects, for example, those with green eyes, 'floating' irises, narrow foreheads, patchy beards, ape-like jaws, and big eyes. If any of these features was ever identified as a definitive indicator of criminality, a lot of people would have to hide their faces forevermore, or go to jail.

There is no one type of face that one can label as the instantly recognisable face of a criminal, but there are some powerful pointers which should serve as warnings.

One is reminded that most murders are committed by people known to the victim, and if you look at photographs of convicted killers (most of whom would never kill again, given their liberty), you will not be likely to detect any pattern of facial characteristics.

Many deeply malicious men and women do have, however, a squint in the right eye. Many also have receding teeth. A common guideline to nastiness and violent, angry reactions are eyebrows shaped like 'ticks' or checkmarks. It is no coincidence that such features are often used and exaggerated by cartoonists for portraying villains.

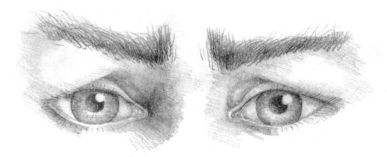

eyebrows like ticks (checkmarks)

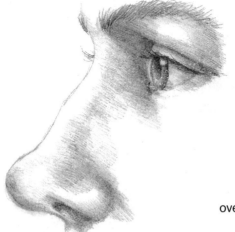

oversized nose tip

Face watchers also know that an oversized nose tip points to violent tendencies in its owner; moreover, the bigger and more bulbous is the nose tip the greater the chances of this person's committing an act of violence.

You may be aware of talk about a person whose behaviour came as a nasty shock. There are numerous instances of violence committed by people who had tight, or seemingly tight, control over their actions and emotions but 'snapped' when their frustration boiled over. You can see the signs building up to this explosion of abnormal violence spreading across the face. Among them are tight, clenched, blanched lips, steely eyes of 'hatred', knitted brows, and shuddering jaws, head and shoulders.

Earlier in this chapter we saw how baby-faced men and women are linked in people's minds with positive qualities and innocence. Could a baby-faced person commit a *violent* crime?

Yes, of course they could. Many murderers have baby faces, yet it is true that those with 'innocent' faces are sometimes considered less accountable for crimes and misdemeanours; their sentences, if they are found guilty, tend to be lighter, which is an indication of how preconceived notions of the meaning of facial appearance can unconsciously influence even trial judges.

CHAPTER 11

REACTIONS AND RESPONSES

The face is a public noticeboard for expressing oneself to the world without using any words. By closely observing faces, you can tell a lot about the people behind the ever-changing facial masks which they unwittingly or intentionally adopt to display their reactions and responses to the events and stimuli around them.

Scientists have attached electrodes to faces to record subtle face movements not easily detected by an observer, but no one needs to invest in machines and electricity cables to be able to identify from facial expressions the principal emotions which human beings display: happiness, surprise, fear, sadness, anger, disgust, interest or attentiveness.

Happiness can, like any emotion, be kept a secret; internalised so to speak. But when it is expressed for all to see it becomes a smiling or laughing face, when the lower eyelids are pushed up by the lower face, wrinkling the skin around the outer corners of the eyes. There is more about smiling and laughing in Chapter 4.

When we are happy our faces and heads are held high, and we are more likely to help others than when we are unhappy or feeling sad. A sad face is distinguished by its eyebrows being drawn together with the inner corners raised. The eyes are often directed downward, the upper lids either tense or, if the person is crying, drooping. Often the lower lip 'falls' down and trembles.

A common and natural response is to show one's sympathy or pity for a distressed person, upon which the sufferer will often break down and cry. You will have noticed, for example, how children burst into tears if you pity them for some small hurt.

Surprise

It can be useful to know if someone is surprised or startled. You might, for instance, confront a person with some news or facts, and wish to discover whether he already knows about it. It is a technique used by many to 'get to the bottom of the matter', or to find out if someone is lying.

Taken by surprise or off guard, a startled person opens his eyes wide, showing the sclera (white area) above and often below the iris. In addition, the eyebrows are raised and held in a curve. The lower jaw 'drops' and the lips part.

Fear reflected on the face also results in wide-open eyes, but the lower lids are tense; the eyebrows are raised, but instead of curving into an arch now they are drawn together. Additionally, the lips are drawn back horizontally.

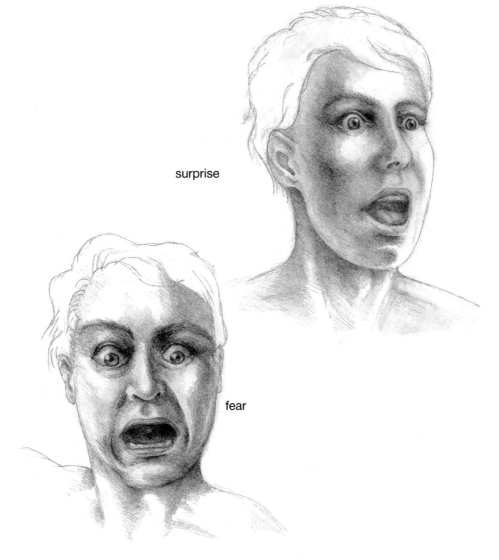

surprise

fear

Anger

Many facial expressions typical of anger are relatively easy to identify. They are:

- lowering and drawing together of the brows;
- direct gaze and probably a strong eye-to-eye contact;
- upper eyelids appear to be lowered, tense and 'square'; and
- lower eyelids tensed and often produce a squint.

anger

Since the days of Aristotle, face watchers have set their sights on the structure of the human face for ways of identifying who among us are bad-tempered and irascible villains. The Greek philosopher decided the giveaway facial characteristic had to be a bulging forehead. The Chinese face readers of the Chin dynasty, twenty-two centuries ago, supported this idea, but added that the bulge had to be most noticeable in the area immediately above the eyebrows. More recent research adds to these findings concerning the forehead, the additional factor of jumping or 'throbbing' veins, which can be seen if an irate person sticks his or her face close to yours.

There are more structural clues to angry dispositions:

- the distance between the tip of the chin and the top of the neck is very short (less than two inches). Outwardly, these individuals appear to be gentle and give in easily rather than engage in an argument. But if they are irritated, they can get very angry indeed;

- very short eyebrows (less than one and a half inches from one end to the other);
- very thick eyelash hairs (which denote a cool disposition but also warn that the person is ferocious when aroused); and
- angry gaze or look in the eyes. This look can be described as a steely glint, cold hatred, a narrowing look of hatred or dark fury. It is the look of many fanatics (political revolutionaries, religious zealots, irate soccer fans, many criminals). And spoilt brats – adults as well as children – can often be identified by this same angry gaze.

Disgust

A disgusted face consists of raised *lower* eyelids and either closed jaws (where the lower lip is pushed up), or open jaws (when the upper lip is raised and the lower lip extended). This expression is sometimes accompanied by a vomiting motion, particularly favoured by children or childlike adults.

A quiet spitting sound, 'Tsk', is used frequently to express disgust or strong disapproval. It is usually accompanied by a wrinkling of the nose as if to protest that something smells horrible.

disgust

EYE CONTACT

If we are interested in another person we will be happy to position our face and body closer than we would to someone we dislike or fear. We will also look more often at their face, thereby signalling our interest in them.

Scientists have filmed what happens when we make eye contact with another person. When we stare at a face, we do not look at the same spot for very long. Our eyes may appear to be focused in a steady gaze, but in reality they are scanning the features of the other's face, concentrating most attention on the mouth and eyes.

Gaze avoidance, or not wanting to make eye contact, is associated with shifty behaviour, suggesting trickery or even dishonesty. But a glance sideways before returning to the other's face is more likely to signal shyness.

You are probably aware of situations in which someone looks away when you expected them to look at you. In all probability their gesture is hostile, cutting you out of their thoughts or simply snubbing you. An experiment devised and conducted by Ralph Exline for American college students in 1966 illustrates this type of hostile reaction. Halfway through an experiment in one psychology class, the students were told their performance was very poor. All reacted by looking less at the experimenter for the remainder of the test, signalling a loss of interest and, possibly, a strong dislike of him.

The eyebrow flash

Where have I seen this person before? His (or her) face is so familiar, but who is he (or she)? All of us have at some time or another been baffled by someone's face, unable to put a name to it.

What most of us may not be aware of, though, is that our unease is compounded if the person we have temporarily 'forgotten' has reacted to us with a subliminal form of greeting which indicates recognition: the eyebrow flash.

The eyebrow flash consists of raising the eyebrows rapidly and momentarily, holding them raised for no more than a sixth of a second.

We are not normally aware how frequently we use or receive the involuntary and sometimes almost imperceptible eyebrow flash, though we will sometimes employ an exaggerated and protracted form of it to draw the attention of a friend in a crowd, or to greet someone we have not seen for a long time – advertising, as it were, the fact that we have recognised them. Women, by emphasising the eyebrows by colouring them and the upper eyelid region immediately beneath the eyebrows, make the eyebrow flash more conspicuous.

The normal response to this facial greeting is to smile back or to answer with an eyebrow flash of our own. But if we receive an eyebrow flash from someone with whom we are not familiar, or whom we have failed to recognise, we are more likely to look away or lower or turn our head.

Although the eyebrow flash is just about universal as a greeting gesture, other reasons for using it differ considerably from culture to culture or person to person. For instance, the Japanese consider it an indecent gesture that should never be made to a person whom one respects. In most countries of Central Europe, it is not used by very reserved, inward-looking adults, while Italians, Spanish, and the 'romantic Latins' of Southern Europe, Central and South America will flash their eyebrows while flirting.

The eyebrow flash is widely practised in Europe and Asia if one is seeking approval or agreement, or beginning a statement in a dialogue. Europeans and people in North America, New Zealand, Australia, and whites in Africa will employ the gesture when strongly disapproving, or thanking, or if they wish to emphasise what they are saying.

Poker-face

A poker face is inscrutable, ideal for not letting anyone know what you are thinking or what your next move will be. Variously described as a stoic expression or a blank look, the poker face is renowned for its zero disclosure.

People with poker faces appear to keep their facial movements to a minimum. They might be aces at poker, bridge or chess, but away from the game they are likely to be very dull, introverted companions.

Still, if you are pitted against a poker-faced opponent and playing for money, any thoughts about companionship will soon seem totally irrelevant. You will have to concentrate all your wits on your opponent's seemingly immobile and expressionless face. There are two ways to penetrate the poker-faced mask: one is directed at your adversary's forehead, and the second is to look closely at the pupils of the eyes.

When a card player or a participant in a competitive game or sport sees a good card or a possible winning move, their pulse points change colour. Before meeting your opponent, you would be well advised to practise on your own face in the privacy of your home the most effective way to locate the positions of the pulse on the side of the forehead (above the temples).

Begin by moving the tips of each index finger over the sides of the forehead, stopping when you feel the pulse beat below. Later, mentally transfer these pulse positions to the face of your opponent: if the

pulse points

adversary is excited the skin above the pulse points turns red or darkens on a pale or white skin, or it glistens and gleams on a brown or black skin. Occasionally you will see the pulse points 'jump' or throb, and then you could be in a lot of trouble because the poker-faced man or woman will be on to a winning streak. However, by reading their pulse points you might be able to do something to save the game, or your wallet, or at least keep your shirt on for the rest of the evening.

The Chinese of Hong Kong spend more money on gambling and race-horses than anyone in the world. It is a well-known fact among Chinese gamblers that the player who has a good set of playing cards must conceal the pupils of his or her eyes because they will probably dilate, and their expansion will let the opponents know that he has a good hand. To conceal this reflex action, many players wear dark glasses.

Jade is considered by the Chinese to be the luckiest and most beautiful stone in the world. They believe that those who wear it close to the heart or gaze upon its eternal beauty will have a good time in the afterlife. Many emperors and empresses were buried in garments made of small pieces of jade. Thousands of years later, today's oriental jade dealers wear dark glasses to hide their eyes, knowing full well that the pupils of their eyes will dilate at the sight of a rare and therefore costly piece of jade, allowing the seller to raise his asking price.

The pupils of the eyes cannot lie, so even if someone with a poker face thinks he or she has your measure, you must check on his progress by looking at his eyes and pulse points, for only by doing this will you know if you are in with a chance of winning.

It is necessary to warn you about the difficulty of seeing whether or not the pupils dilate, particularly in a dark room or in any poor light. And so, if your eyes are dark brown or black, chances are that your opponents will not be able to see your pupils or read their movement accurately. However, if you have blue or green, grey or very pale brown eyes you can bet your bottom dollar, pound, franc or mark that everyone will be able to

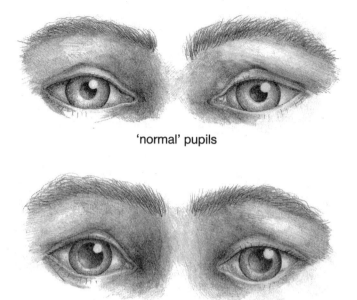

'normal' pupils

dilated pupils

read your face if you are dealt the perfect prize-winning set of cards. The moral of this tale is simply this: those with pale-coloured eyes should not expect to make their fortune by gambling.

In America, an experiment was conducted on pupil dilation – with extremely fascinating results. Apparently the Don Juan type of men, who chase after a lot of women and boast about the number of conquests they make, showed a clear preference for women with constricted (small) pupils over those with dilated (large) pupils. This seemed surprising, since the women with dilated pupils would be those most thrilled and excited by them. The conclusion reached was that the Don Juan might be fearful of a fawning woman who might be intent on forming a long-term relationship; or, another explanation as I see it, could be that, having detected from the enlarged state of her pupils that the woman was already aroused, he preferred to abandon her and set off to find another whose tight pupils showed that she represented a greater challenge.

In another American experiment, groups of men and women were shown photographs of babies. Both groups were divided into single, married, parents and childless. The majority of women in all groups reacted with dilated pupils, signalling pleasure or excitement at the sight of a baby. The result was very different for the men; only those who were already parents responded with dilated eyes.

GIVE ME TIME TO THINK

There are occasions on which we have to play for time before making a decision: shall I tell my wife that I lost my wallet and credit cards or wait for her to find out? Shall I tell him he looks awful in his dinner jacket because it is too tight for him? Should I discard the five of hearts or keep it and hope the king will turn up?

Decisions, decisions, but it can be useful to know if someone is stalling for time, especially if their final decision or announcement has an important effect on you.

Some of the most effective facial gestures commonly employed to buy a short time-to-think or breathing space in conversation are:

- taking off your spectacles and putting the earpiece end into the mouth;
- putting an object such as the end of a pen into the mouth so that you cannot speak clearly;
- dropping your spectacles on to the centre of the nose and peering over them. This is effective if you intend to upset another person;
- stroking your chin or tugging at your beard;
- squinting slightly as if you are looking into the future;
- rubbing your nose, a gesture of puzzlement and 'Let me think about it'; and
- lifting one eyebrow (which is also a gesture associated with artistic thoughts and creativity).
- exclamations of 'I give up, but if you give me time I'll try to come up with an answer', or 'Pouf', a mild French expletive which reproduces in other languages as a movement in which the lower lip protrudes and then clamps over the upper lip, the mouth thrusts forward, and the facial expression can be accompanied by placing the hands open with the palms up, or shrugging the shoulders, or doing shoulder and hand movements simultaneously.

WOULD YOU BUY A SECONDHAND CAR FROM THIS PERSON?

The salesman or woman has three tried-and-tested techniques to urge you to buy a product. First, they ask for the moon, but are prepared to settle for less. By lowering the price they can make you believe you are getting a bargain.

Secondly, they get you to agree to purchase a relatively small or inexpensive product, then tempt you with a bigger or more expensive one. Or, they try to get you to buy something, and while you are thinking about it they offer something else as bait. For example, 'We have a special offer on this car of five per cent off the advertised price if you pay cash. And because *you* have an honest face I'll give you a year's road tax, and for good measure I'll throw in two spare tyres, Michelin of course!' This sales technique is called 'that's not all'.

So, you have listened to the sales pitch. What, if anything, can you tell from looking at a salesperson's face? Heavy pressure to make you buy is normally accompanied by a bright, forced smile and wide-opened eyes in a 'do-or-die' effort. A gentle gaze or look in the eyes suggests a cooperative approach to the idea of making you purchase his product. A slight smile signals 'I'm not trying to make you do something you might regret'.

The sales talk might be fast or persuasive, or a slow explanation delivered with a conspiratorial demeanour, often with reduced lip movement. This latter approach is in the manner of 'I'll do this specially for you, but no one else'.

If you appear uninterested or hesitant, their manner will turn into '*You'd* be a fool to resist this offer', accompanied by a confident smile and eye contact.

At this point, they know and *you* should know that if they apply too much pressure by fast talk or more forced smiles, you will back away because you feel you are about to lose your freedom of choice. Moreover, they know and so should you that by offering too large a reward or bait, they are making the product seem more attractive and superior to its real worth. So, your suspicions aroused, you wonder what is wrong with this product, you back away and no sale is made.

It may assist you in your role as a prospective buyer or if you intend to follow a sales career to know what a salesperson sees in the face of a potential customer. A successful salesman or woman has to be good at reading faces.

Customer's face	What the salesperson sees
• face turned away	shutting out the salesperson
• eyes look down	shutting out the salesperson
• makes eye contact with the salesperson and holds it for a few seconds	there might be a sale here
• eye contact held a few seconds, plus a faint smile or smirk	there is a good chance of making a sale here
• mouth relaxed, chin forward, no forced (faked) smile	the customer is interested
• relaxed smile, head and face held high or straight, confident gaze (eyes)	the customer is on the point of buying/agreeing to the sale

And finally, how can you, the customer, identify the skilful, persuasive manipulators by their faces rather than by their sales talk?

There are two types of mouths associated with charm, cleverness, intelligence, persuasion and subtle influence. Used or secondhand car dealers might well have either or both features, but you should be warned that the owner of either characteristic of the mouth is not necessarily dishonest or manipulative. He or she could be an ideal person in advertising, the media, public relations, or in a stage or film career.

For the record, then, the two mouths of persuasion are:

- an upward-curving line formed where the lips meet when the mouth is in repose. This curved line also indicates creativity.
- a pointed mouth in which the lips meet to form a point at the centre (visible in profile).

pointed mouth

LYING

Face watchers are in luck if they want to know who is telling a lie because the face is a dead giveaway if its owner is lying. The telltale signs to look for are made easy because those hoping to deceive pay more attention to what they say than what they do with their faces and bodies. Here are the principal signs:

- bites lower lip (nervous, when lying);
- plays with own hair or earrings (nervous before an interview for a job at which the candidate might have to exaggerate or lie about his or her qualities or qualifications);
- rigid or controlled face trying hard not to give anything away;

- self-consciously covers mouth before answering a question;
- voice pitch goes higher; voice sounds more negative, less fluid;
- makes vague, sweeping statements;
- gestures increase, for example, touches the face, plays with spectacles;
- blink rate increases (a sign of nervousness);
- avoids eye contact or looks at you sideways 'out of the corner of the eye';
- looks away (nervously) before responding; or
- smiles, but leans face away from you.

When children tell lies they produce even more giveaway signals, among them:

- avoiding looking at the adult or questioner;
- covering mouth *while* speaking;
- looking down;
- the face twitches;
- wetting their lips;
- a lot of throat clearing;
- rubbing the nose; and
- scratching the head or face while talking.

Some of us never grow up, retaining childlike qualities for life. So it is possible that adult liars will produce some of the giveaways in the children's list. American psychologists find that children have the hardest task lying to parents, but are very successful at lying to grandparents.

A couple of years ago, I entered the Red Channel at London airport after an overnight flight from New York. After declaring a couple of cameras and lenses, a portable radio and a portable CD player, I paid the import duty imposed by the customs and excise officer, who then asked a surprising question.

'Have you anything else to declare that I should know about?'

Insulted, I told him angrily that if I had wanted to lie about the type and quantity of taxable items brought back from America, why then would I have chosen to enter the Red Channel to declare them when I could have opted for the Green Channel through which you enter if you have 'nothing to declare'. His reply was an eye-opener.

Some of the world's best smugglers enter the Red Channel. They declare some goods, pay the import duty, and hope to get away with a fistful of diamonds or a quantity of heroin with a street value of millions of pounds. He went on to say that he could tell by my face that I was not a liar or a smuggler.

Is there a moral in this tale? Yes, that some of the world's best customs and excise officers can read your face, so watch it!

HONEST OR DISHONEST?

That great Dame of the English theatre, Sybil Thorndike, once declared herself to be a first-class liar, adding with refreshing candour that maybe there was some kind of link with the fact that she had been brought up in the household of a clergyman. When put to the test, each of us will act dishonestly at least once in a lifetime.

It is easier to pick out a dishonest person than an honest one when looking at the faces of a crowd of total strangers. Undoubtedly dishonest and devious are those with eyes that curve up from the inner corner by the nose like a new crescent moon, descending smoothly to the outer corner by the side of the face. Owners of new moon eyes also have an extremely strong sex drive, which is explained in more detail in Chapter 8.

Unless they are victims of an accident or debilitated by a stroke or another medical condition, those with a crooked nose or a crooked mouth are powerfully motivated to cheat, deceive and act deviously whenever it suits them.

However, that is not to say that everyone possessing these facial characteristics will always act dishonestly. The chances are that they will be less ethical, more shameless, and will tell more lies if they think they can get away with it. 'It' can be as minor as finding a dollar bill on a sidewalk and pocketing it instead of handing it in to the nearest police station, or as major as diverting the blame from themselves to another for some malfeasance of their own doing.

It may not surprise you to learn that a large number of world leaders and politicians in the Nineties have crooked mouths, a characteristic especially apparent when they are speaking or being interviewed on television. Some rogues are likeable, but anyone whose crooked nose is distinguished by ending in a pointed tip is nasty, spiteful, and to be feared (see page 165).

'His mouth is honey, his heart a sword' warned a Persian scholar in the days of the last Shah of Iran, after studying the ruler's face. Skilful and dishonest in argument, glib-tongued and quite nonchalant about it all are those whose upper lip is, like the Shah's was, thicker by far than the lower lip. This type of mouth can be found among top political leaders of every period in the history of the world.

It is not easy to tell who is totally honest. Thousands of face watchers have, during the last fifty or sixty years, attributed such facial features as a round nose tip, and a heavy beard growth in the centre of the chin to an honest disposition. While there is no evidence that either trait points out an honest man or woman, there are three unusual and thought-provoking characteristics which are worth considering as possible clues to honesty; they are:

- a mole situated at the outer corner of the eye;
- big cheeks that are neither gross nor flabby, but are generously 'meaty'. (Additionally, owners of these cheeks need more sleep than most. If they are overtaken by a violent reversal of fortune or by a shattering event, they recover slowly, or may stay down forever).
- as likely as any to be honest are those who will look you straight in the eye and say: 'I don't know', instead of bluffing.

US OR THEM?

If you are French or Scottish and you pat the head of a neighbour's son, you are making a friendly gesture and probably have a satisfactory relationship with the people living next door.

If you were to pat the head of a child, teenager, or anyone at all in Thailand, your gesture would be taken as an insult, degrading to the other person and causing him or her to lose face.

Every year millions of people travel to a foreign country on business, to visit relatives and friends, or for their vacations. All of us make mistakes, putting our foot into it because we are not aware of cultural differences and local attitudes or practices.

Many embarrassing errors and dreadful *faux pas* inadvertently committed by travellers abroad concern the face. Since no one likes to lose face, or to be insulted to their face, there now follows a selection of facial gestures and an explanation of their significance in various parts of the world. Although the list is not a complete one, it could be useful to anyone planning visits to the countries included in this selection.

Head and Face

Pat the head of someone; tousle someone's hair	<ul><li>a friendly gesture</li><li>to insult or degrade someone</li></ul>	<ul><li>Western countries</li><li>Thailand, Burma, Fiji, Indonesia, Singapore</li></ul>
Hit one's forehead with open palm	<ul><li>exasperation</li></ul>	<ul><li>Western countries</li></ul>
Rock the head gently side to side	<ul><li>'Yes, I'm listening'</li></ul>	<ul><li>India, Bangladesh</li></ul>

Nod the head up and down	• to indicate 'yes'	• most countries
Nod the head up and down	• to indicate 'no'	• most of Greece, India and Bangladesh; Bulgaria, Serbia, Iran, Turkey, Sri Lanka
Shake the head side to side	• to indicate 'yes'	

Chin flick: brush the backs of the fingers under the chin then outward	• 'I don't know the answer'	• Portugal, Brazil, Argentina
	• to signal impatience or disgust	• Italy
	• 'Go away! You're a pest'	• France
	• an insulting gesture	• Tunisia

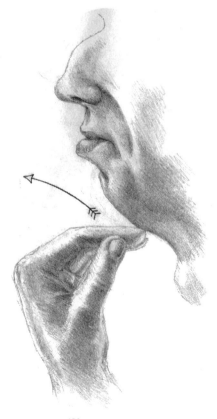

Jerk the chin up	• to indicate 'no'	• North Africa, Malta, Ghana, Greece, southern Italy, Turkey
	• to indicate 'yes'	• India
	• 'Come here, I've something to tell you'	• Australia, Germany, Scandinavia
	• 'I've forgotten'	• Paraguay
Nod the head backwards while clicking the tongue	• to indicate 'no'	• Saudi Arabia, Dubai, Abu Dhabi, Yemen, Somalia, northern Egypt, Tunisia, Bulgaria
Tap the forehead near the temple or pulse points	• to indicate that someone is very intelligent, or has a lot of common sense	• Western Europe; English-speaking countries
	• 'I'm thinking about it' and 'Leave it to me'	• South America; English-speaking countries
Rotate the index finger against the temple or pulse points	• 'He/she is crazy!' 'A screw loose!'	• English-speaking countries; Bulgaria
Tap the middle of one's forehead	• 'He/she is crazy!'	• Holland, parts of Indonesia, South Africa

Eyes

Avoid eye contact	• as a general practice	• Africa, Caribbean
	• as a gesture of respect or deference	• Britain; North America, Japan, Ghana, South Africa

Avoid eye contact (continued)	• by women in order to avoid a suggestion of romantic interest, if men are present	• Zambia, Colombia, Mali, Turkey and Moslem countries
	• embarrassment	• England
Stare at someone	• the only way to find out something	• China, Taiwan, Saudi Arabia, Pakistan
Do not stare at others	• because it is rude	• Britain; Japan, Ireland, Thailand, Korea, Australia, New Zealand, Western Europe, North America, Zimbabwe
Winking	• 'I'm in the know' and 'We share a secret'	• North America, Ireland, Australia, New Zealand, Western Europe
	• impolite gesture	• Hong Kong
	• flirtatious signal	• Western countries
	• 'I'm not serious. I'm kidding'	• North America, Britain, Australia
Touch the outer corner of the eye	• 'I know what you're up to'. 'You can't fool me'	• France, Britain
	• 'Take care. Be alert'	• Italy
	• expression of disappointment	• Croatia, Bosnia, Serbia, Albania
Remove sunglasses when entering a home or if speaking to someone	• because it is impolite to look at someone with 'dark eyes'	• Indonesia, South Korea, Japan

Quick jerky movements behind closed eyelids	• dreaming	• universal

Nose

| Tap the nose | • 'I know, but don't tell anyone' | • Britain |
| | • 'Look out! Take care!' | • Italy |

| Wrinkle the nose | • if there is a bad smell | • Western countries |
| | • expression of disgust | • Western countries |

| Thumb the nose | • to insult, mock or jeer at another | • nearly universal |

Pinch the nose	• if there is a bad smell	• nearly universal
	• if a scheme, project or product is seen as a failure	• North America, Britain, Australia, New Zealand
Make a circle with thumb and index finger and put it over the nose	• to indicate that 'someone there is drunk'	• France
Push the nose up with the index and middle finger	• 'It's so easy that I can do it with the fingers stuck up my nose'	• France
Blow one's nose	• to clear it	• widespread
	• only in private, never in public, because it is considered rude	• Korea, Japan
	• never at the dinner table because it is rude	• Malaysia

Cheeks

Rotate index finger into the cheek	• to signal admiration; for example, when a beautiful girl walks past	• Italy
	• 'That's crazy!'	• Germany

Ears

Flick or touch the ear lobe	• to signal that another person is gay or effeminate	• Italy

Tug and squeeze one's own ear lobe	• apologise to superiors for an error; e.g. breaking a glass object	• India
	• submission, e.g. younger brother to older brother	• India
	• as a self-punishment for a misdemeanour; e.g. a child speaks out of turn in the school classroom	• India
	• to express appreciation	• Brazil
The index finger makes circular motions around the ear	• to signal that someone or something is crazy or stupid	• North America
	• to signal to someone 'You're wanted on the telephone'	• South America, Holland, South Africa

Cup an ear with one hand	• 'I can't hear you'	• nearly universal

Mouth

Stick out the tongue	• to mock or deride someone	• English-speaking countries
	• an involuntary sign of concentration	• universal
	• to greet a friend	• Tibet
Giggle	• amusement	• universal
	• sexual frustration	• universal
	• embarrassment – women often cover their mouths with the hand or a piece of clothing when they giggle	• China, Taiwan, Hong Kong, Japan, Malaysia, India, Bangladesh, Pakistan, Philippines, Singapore, Nepal, Tibet
Slowly lick the lips	• sexual invitation	• widespread
	• 'I'm hungry' (for food)	• English-speaking countries
Blow on an imaginary flute	• to signal that someone is too talkative or boring	• France
Cover the mouth with a white gauze mask	• in a hospital operating theatre	• nearly universal
	• fear of air pollution	• China; cyclists in Western countries
	• to prevent passing germs to others	• Japan

Spitting	• to insult someone by spitting in their face or in the general direction of the body	• nearly universal
	• a 'natural' way of expelling body waste by spitting on to floors, pavements, or into spittoons (receptacle) located in public places	• China
	• to express a liking for someone by spitting on their feet	• Masai tribe, Kenya; parts of Sudan
Cover the mouth with the hand	• to politely cover a yawn	• widespread
	• because it is rude to display an open mouth on all occasions, e.g. cover the mouth when laughing or using a toothpick	• Chinese, Japanese, Thai, Indonesian, Burmese, and Korean women
Against eating in the street	• vulgar	• France; Poland
Against using fingers to eat with	• unnecessary; vulgar	• France; Japan; Bolivia
Purse the lips and point with the mouth at an object	• because it is rude to point with the finger	• Philippines

This is as good a moment as any to give advice to anyone who is planning to do business in Asian countries, in particular Thailand, China and Japan. Never show or express anger by raising your voice or displaying it on your face. Quiet explanation or discussion of a problem will probably induce the company's representative to sign the contract and do business with you, but any shouts, swearing or cursing will fall on deaf ears. If you display anger in these countries *you* will lose face, not the man or woman who is the target of your temper. The same rules apply to tourists: if you shout or lose your temper the hotel employee will not cooperate, and then *you* will feel murderous.

M CHAPTER 12
OODY BLUES

WARNING: Parts of this chapter are blue. And it is going to get bluer as you turn the pages because it will take a look at the type of people most susceptible to 'blue' moods or likely to induce the blues in other people. We will also consider the faces of the men and women whose moody behaviour adversely affects and dispirits others, causing ill humour and antipathetic reaction all round: at home, at work, in close personal relationships, or with neighbours and acquaintances.

On the optimistic side it could be said that moody blues need not endure forever. If you identify yourself in this chapter, you are advised to consult Chapter 7, for there are set out a number of ideas and suggestions for making friends and influencing your moods for the better.

ARGUMENTATIVE, ARROGANT, AUTHORITARIAN

'I like talking to a brick wall, it's the only thing in the world that never contradicts me'. The words are from Oscar Wilde's pen, but the sentiments will be familiar to those given to arguing or playing the devil's advocate – the man or woman who enjoys speaking in favour of an unpopular or opposing view, often for the sake of an argument.

You probably know or meet people who will tenaciously cling to their side of an argument, even if they know they are wrong. Rather than lose face or lose the argument, they hurl insults and abuse, unable to break off and give up when they are beaten. The person hurt most in a bruising verbal encounter is often someone they like or love most.

You must look at the ears first, then the mouth and chin to identify the candidate whose attitude or technique best fits the bossy, imperious method of argument as in: 'Shut up!' he explained. They are:

- the tragus shows prominently when the person is seen full face;
- the area between the nose and upper lip protrudes and the philtrum is at least one inch wide (see page 14). These characteristics also reveal their owners' profound fear of failure, especially in their career and in making friends.

chin joins lower lip
in a 'straight' line

Arrogant and argumentative is the person whose chin joins the lower lip in a straight line, instead of the customary concave depression that is a feature of most chins. Hubristic, too, are those with:

- small indents or 'dimples' in each corner of the mouth (which also signal impatience and superciliousness); and
- an extremely wide nose, with bulbous sides and a plump, bulging nose tip.

Arrogance is an attitude of those who frequently raise their eyebrows, retaining them in this elevated position when they lift their heads in a backward movement, eyelids lowered, to cut off contact with another person. In fact, this series of facial movements constitutes a factual 'No' in Greek. In both examples, the message is unfriendly, and can be taken to mean 'keep your distance'.

The sneer expression (see page 161), where the nose wings and top lip wrinkle or gather up while vertical creases appear down the ridge of the nose, is a facial presentation that signals arrogance, indignation, and a fundamental desire to find faults in everything.

AGGRESSION

Without a certain amount of aggression we would be trampled on, taken advantage of, or ignored in this greatly competitive world. Men are more aggressive than women. They commit the most violent crimes. They are the football hooligans. Most societies – primitive and developed – tolerate, even encourage, aggression in males but not females; boys are given toy guns, men are the hunters, the marines and the paratroopers.

Women generally feel more guilty and anxious about behaving aggressively, and are more worried about the possible dangers to themselves arising from their aggression. Female aggression is mostly verbal, and is intended to inflict psychological pain.

When frustration is the cause of aggression, a common reaction is for the subjects to throw their hands in the air with the palms up, tilt their head back, then make a facial grimace and a muttered 'Huh'. Or, they mouth silently, or shout, one of the famous four-letter words.

There are plenty of opportunities for frustration at work and in family life. Dissatisfaction with one's job, conflicts between supervisors and workers, a sense of being under-valued or over-worked are common causes of aggressive feelings, which must necessarily be concealed by most would-be aggressors if they are to retain their jobs.

So, you see plenty of resentful looks and oaths muttered under the breath, many pursed lips, and a gaze or look in the eyes of barely concealed rage.

At home, frustrated aggressors will exhibit similar facial signals, but freed from the constraints of having to 'behave' in front of colleagues and bosses they are likely to be louder and more obviously on the offensive.

Pain increases aggression. That is evidenced in the pursed lips of the 'grin-and-bear-it' attitude to suffering, where the would-be aggressor is making a visible effort to contain a natural inclination to hit back. Other facial evidence of pain, which should be treated as a warning signal of a probably more aggressive mood to follow, is the 'ouch' grimace, visible when the subject is stricken by a flash of pain. Or, those in pain will be seen to suck in air through clenched teeth, hold their breath and release it with a quick 'Ach'.

Hot weather, with high temperatures and high humidity, contributes to aggression. Perspiration dripping down the face, or red, flushed cheeks are the most common facial distress signs. And outbursts of anger and short tempers are noticeable before the rains and monsoons come in tropical lands, or before the long, dark days and nights of the polar winters.

Before I give an extended list of more facial signs that tell of aggression, it is important to mention the effects of *passive* aggression, first identified during the First World War when soldiers began to resist or ignore orders.

Passive aggressives, according to the textbooks, retreat into themselves, convinced that they have been unfairly treated. They are determined to get even with everyone, including of course the authorities, by stealth. They are inclined to put others in the wrong, painting themselves as the victim.

The telltale signs of aggressive, combative men and women include the use of facial gestures and expressions, and the presence of certain facial structures, in particular in the areas of the chin and jaw. Look out for these facial qualities:

- an exaggerated square jaw of a bully, with the chin thrust forward, teeth clenched, depicted by cartoonists as: the battle-axe face of a mother-in-law; or the face of the 'typical' army disciplinarian, glowering at a trembling recruit;
- projecting lower lip and upper chin (see page 165). The owner of this facial development believes that might is right, resorting to force if possible to solve an argument when words have failed; and
- visible eyebrow *roots*, possible if the hairs grow or lie in a certain conspicuous direction (you will see it instantly if the phenomenon is present).

Bossy, quarrelsome and constantly seeking to impose their will are those whose faces possess at least two of the distinctive characteristics which follow:

- one or both ear lobes *attached* to the cheek, without a slit or clear-cut edge which would otherwise enable the lower part of the lobe to hang independently by the side of the face;

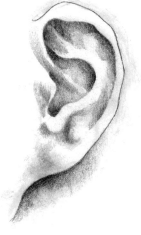

ear lobe 'attached'
to the cheek

- one or both eyes are triangular in shape, resembling the hooded look of a crow that can silence all comers by 'the look' that can kill. This is the superior eye for a political career, with many top leaders possessing this visual quality. If the eyelid droops *very* noticeably, be warned that you are dealing with an interfering busybody;

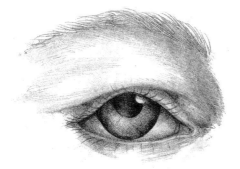

triangular eye

- 'toned' or robust skin;
- a large nose – that is, long and wide, wide nostrils, broad nostril wings, high sides, big nose tip; and
- frequently jerks up the chin, accompanied by an uttered 'Tsk'/'Tchk'

Especially *peevish* and *crusty* are the men whose eyebrows grow long and bushy and hang over their eyes like protruding broomheads. This phenomenon occurs in middle-aged and elderly men, though rarely in women.

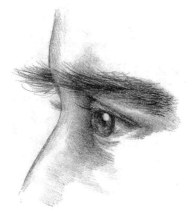

protruding broomhead
eyebrows

Authoritarians can count among their distinguishing facial features and expressions most of the factors associated with bossiness, aggression and arrogance. Authoritarians are people who have an exaggerated need to submit to, and identify with, strong authority.

They adhere rigidly to conventional values and patterns of behaviour, favouring harsh punishment for anyone deviating from their idea of 'normal' practices. They tend to lack a sense of humour, or so it would appear to those with a less conventional moral outlook.

Authoritarians despise weaker people, especially members of minority groups. They will be heard frequently laying down the law: 'A person has no breeding if he eats with his fingers'; and 'Respect and obedience to our parents and elders are the most important virtues that most of us have forgotten'.

Authoritarians share with *autocrats* (who are the real dictators) a strong urge to shut out or turn a deaf ear to any opposition. It is not uncommon for autocrats and authoritarians to have very long chins, and if they do they will probably be the warmer, more humane type with whom you can work without being made to feel downtrodden or drained of liberty. However, those with long chins expect, and exact, the total loyalty of dependents, supporters and followers, so if you disagree with them you are advised to think the matter or argument through before daring to draw attention to it or yourself.

Two characteristics which go with an autocratic or authoritarian type are:

- very thick eyebrows; and
- a very big, bulbous nose tip, which also warns that the owner of the bulge can be violent.

Many of the individuals identified so far in this chapter are extremely *narrow-minded* and *intolerant*. The face watcher can separate the moderately narrow-minded from the autocrats by studying the ears. For example, those whose ear length is about twice the measure of the width will be moderately intolerant of racial minorities, unmarried mothers, drug addicts or political dissenters. These long-eared men and women are the type of person who can be heard to say at an art exhibition or the first night at the opera: 'I simply can't understand why all the fuss is being made over this peculiar painting/dreadful modern music/strange native exhibit.'

People with this level of intolerance are usually quite harmless, although they can be irritating to broad-minded liberals. In fact, a narrow-minded person can put to the test not only a saint but also *your* degree of tolerance, too.

Most of us are *tense* while we sit in the dentist's waiting room or in his chair. We get *anxious* too, while waiting to be called into an important interview or while we stand around in the departure lounge at an airport. And we feel anxious if we do not know a single face at a gathering of animatedly conversing strangers.

A great many will yawn, not because they are bored but rather, it is something to do with those self-conscious hands and speechless mouths which contribute to their feelings of anxiety, tension and social clumsiness.

Fearful people want to be with others in the same situation, to take their minds off the problem. 'Can you tell me if this is the nine-thirty train for Paris?' they will ask, as a pretext to stand near you. Reassured, the tautness around their mouth and the anxious, almost haunted look in their eyes, diminish. They need to be among 'friendly' faces.

The anxious gravitate, if there is a choice, towards someone with knowledge: a woman who is having her first baby will probably choose to share a room with or sit beside someone who has had one before, rather than approach another first-timer. In addition to a perceptible relaxation of the muscles around the eyes and mouth, a sigh of relief through relaxed or smiling lips signals a reduction of tension and apprehension.

More anxiety signals involve the mouth, among them:

- clearing the throat because a 'frog' is obstructing it (the French call this build-up of mucus *un chat dans la gorge*, a cat in the throat);
- swallowing a lot (either because of mucus or the throat feels dry);
- sucking the thumb, fingers, toy, top of a pen (any of which might be thought of as a mother's breast or bottle substitute);
- puffing on a cigar, cigarette, or pipe;
- biting the nails; or
- grinding one's teeth during sleep.

Other visual evidence of tension incorporates hand-to-face gestures such as:

- supporting the chin or propping up the face;
- rubbing the cheek;
- touching the mouth; and
- resting the brow in the palm of the hand, which is usually a male gesture.

It is worth noting that these four hand-to-face gestures are also signs of boredom.

No matter how hard anxious and depressed individuals try to hide their discomfort or pain, their faces will betray their emotions. The face watcher should therefore look for, or take note of, these physical conditions and complaints:

- frequent migraines, headaches;
- stiff neck;
- dark patches under the eyes, though if these are temporary they suggest a poor night's rest or sleeplessness; and

- lines or creases that slant from the nose ridge down the sides of the nose to give a pinched-nose look

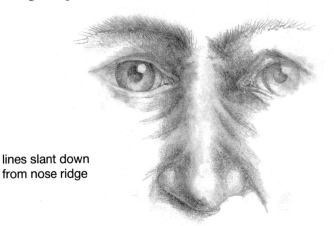

lines slant down
from nose ridge

Advertisers address themselves to 'the depressed, the low in spirits, and those down in the dumps' with a view to selling them a cupboardful of little and large pills, lotions and potions, capsules and inhalants.

Charles Darwin closely observed his friends, family and in particular, his children, in his search for the origins of emotional responses and facial expressions, recording in his notebooks for example the facial signs of *depression*. These are some of his jottings:

- 'corners of the mouth depressed';
- 'inner corner of the eyebrows raised by that muscle which the French call the "grief muscle"';
- 'eyebrows become slightly oblique, with a little swelling at the inner end'; and
- 'the forehead is transversely wrinkled in the middle part, but not across the whole breadth as when the eyebrows are raised in surprise.'

Experimental work carried out at Liverpool University shows that those with depression are much more realistic about their lives and capabilities than are happy people. In June 1992, a psychologist from the Liverpool research team wrote in the *Journal of Medical Ethics* that normal people overestimate the amount of control they have over events, while depressed people are better in many ways at judging what other people think of them.

A degree of depression, then, may contribute a helpful element of realism to one's outlook, but there is also the risk that depression will make us moody and resentful.

Resentful people are those who are discontented with their lot in life. They include those who detest having regularly to perform their domestic chores, or being obliged to submit to the directions of others. They are sulky and irritable. Similarly discontented and restless are those with itchy feet, people who want to be somewhere else or doing something completely different. The signs of resentfulness, rebelliousness and also sulkiness are these:

- crow's feet (lines radiating out from the outer corners of the eyes) on a person aged thirty-five or under;
- a vertical line/crease rising from the area between the eyebrows up through the middle of the forehead to end at the hairline;
- a jagged/ragged hairline; and
- a permanently pouting mouth (which is also a sign of a bad-tempered person).

Not many people are naturally or genuinely charming. Charmers depend on the appreciation of other people, many behaving as outrageously as they think is necessary in order to be favourably noticed.

Oscar Wilde thought the secret of all charming people was that they are spoiled. Albert Camus had a similar diagnosis of the charm condition, describing it as a way of hearing the answer 'yes' without ever having asked a question.

The trouble with *inconsistency*, such as being charming one moment and unpleasant the next, is that you never know what mood your unpredictable friend will be in from one day to the next. Be warned, if you are still making up your mind whether or not to commit yourself to someone in a long-term relationship that there are a few facial signs to alert you to inconsistent conduct:

- a cleft/split/slit running up the centre (ridge) of the nose from the nose tip;

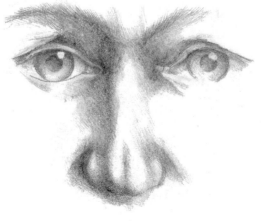

cleft or 'slit'
at nose tip

- 'gappy' teeth (wide gaps between teeth);
- blotchy/stained complexion;
- a nose with a very long/elongated nose tip;

elongated tip

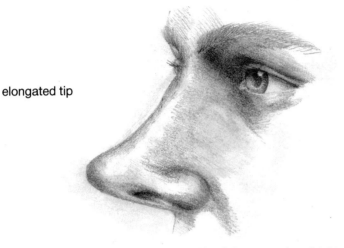

- short, untidy eyebrows (especially if they are also thick).

short, untidy
eyebrow

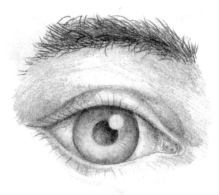

Many people whose faces possess one or more of these traits will also act out of control, at times. That is to say they will blurt out hurtful things to a loved one, and at the end of the explosion and barrage of angry words they will have completely 'forgotten' what injustices (or truths) they have uttered. Then they wonder why the target of their abuse is a crumpled figure, demolished by the explosion of uncontrollable behaviour.

Impulsive are those who cannot stop to reflect, analyse, or weigh the pros and cons before acting. This sudden inclination to act can be refreshing at times; for instance, if someone suggests an impromptu picnic on a fine, sunny Sunday morning. But impulsive people can get into trouble, too. Sometimes their gut reactions or enthusiasm overwhelm their judgement, as when they rush out to buy a new shares issue without first asking how the company or corporation has performed in the months preceding the offer.

Impulsiveness is apparent from these facial characteristics:

- middle of the forehead bulges (convex) like a baby's, or the forehead slants *acutely* from eyebrow level to the hairline (NB: a *moderately* slanting forehead denotes decisiveness);
- a big mouth with thick lips; and
- eyebrow ends (nearest the side of the head) rise.

eyebrow
end rises

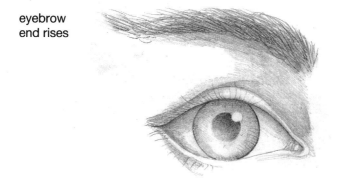

While moody blues can cause their owner a lot of ups and downs and periods of suffering and acute depression, it has to be said that a great many moody individuals cause their friends and loved ones to have moody blues, too. Bad moods are infectious, but it is also possible to be depressed by other people's irrepressible cheerfulness, a tiring habit of many who see themselves as the life and soul of the party. Another type of individual can cause a bad attack of the moody blues: the insouciant.

Insouciant people are largely carefree and unconcerned, indifferent to most of what is happening around them. They can induce immense unhappiness in those at the receiving-end of their 'I don't give a damn' attitude. Self-contained to the core, and heedless of the concerns and anxieties of others, insouciant men and women cannot understand why their partner assails them with complaints of 'You don't understand me' or 'You don't care about me'.

There are two important facial signs which show those who adopt a self-contained, insouciant attitude to life. The first is a small, undeveloped tragus (see page 116). The second indicator is a small mouth, but take heed: those with small mouths are individuals who are liable to bottle up and hide their problems, or deny they have any. Their apparent self-control and lack of concern may break down if ever those problems suddenly become overwhelming.

Indifferent are those who readily make the 'I don't care' type of gesture with their mouth – corners down, the mouth arches up, and the bottom lip is pushed forward. The mouth shrug is frequently, but not necessarily, accompanied by a matching eyebrow shrug, a sideways tilt of the head, and a shrug of the shoulders as an involuntary imitation of the mouth shrug.

Selfishness is a nose-length away from the behavioural traits so far mentioned in this section. The facial signs include droopy eyelids and very thick eyebrows, but you should also be aware of these telltale pieces of evidence:

- triangular-shaped eyebrows (see page 61);
- extremely thin lips (but selfishness is offset if the person's nose tip is round);
- nose tip which turns down acutely towards the mouth (this also indicates meanness and untrustworthy tendencies); and
- thin ears with pointed tops.

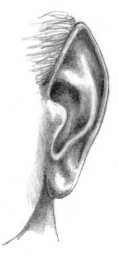

thin ear with
pointed top

One of the most stimulating and rewarding aspects of reading faces is the ease with which you can tell at a glance if someone is *patient* or *impatient*. How fortunate are those who are paired to a patient man or woman; life with an impatient partner may be exciting in the early stages, but as the years go by, having to react to someone who cannot stand still, who 'suffers' if he or she is kept waiting, must require the perseverance and endurance of those most patient of stalkers – the lioness, the heron, and the human fisherman, in particular the angler.

Here, then are the vital clues which will allow you to identify patient and impatient individuals.

Patient
* when the nostrils are straight/level

straight
nostrils

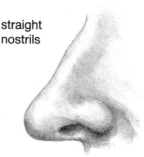

Quite patient
* when the nostrils point down. These individuals are relatively patient and not easily ruffled. If they are severely provoked, however, they can explode with frightening strength and venom

nostrils
point down

Impatient
* when the nostrils slant up, as if something is getting up their nose, causing an irritation. Their impatience is exacerbated if the nostrils are big;
* when the eyebrows grow very close to the eyes;
* those who nod their heads vigorously to signal impatience. This is often accompanied by 'Yes, yes', or sighs. You may have noticed that impatient television interviewers frequently interrupt their guests or interviewees with 'Yes, but . . .'

nostrils
slant up

So, thank you for your patience while delving into the secrets of the face in these pages about the moody blues. On impatience, though, the last thoughts come from the Spanish-born American philosopher, George Santayana, who observed that patience is needed to know the value of domestic bliss, while unhappiness is preferred by volatile spirits.

CHAPTER 13

Six Famous Faces

Princess of Wales

The Princess of Wales is famous for her radiant smile, which bears all the hallmarks of warmth and friendliness, and she has certainly beguiled large numbers of men, women and children of many nations.

Her face, like her public image, is finely groomed, with the best features skilfully highlighted to present to the world at large a sincere and very attractive appearance. With so much dressing-up, can the perceptive face watcher see through the public face to glimpse the real princess behind the mask and regal tiara?

That she is a gifted communicator is attested by the three zones of her face: her middle zone (eyebrows to nose tip) is longer than either her forehead (top zone) or her low zone (nose tip to chin), an important middle zone signalling an individual who is clever at projecting a good self-image and gifted with a flair for public relations. However, her modestly proportioned forehead discloses a moderate intellect, and that she is a do-er rather than a thinker.

Her power can never be under-estimated, though, for a chin which protrudes as forcefully as hers demonstrates that when its owner is bent on attaining something or someone, he or she will succeed. President John F. Kennedy and Jacqueline Kennedy Onassis are among the few famous individuals whose chins could rival the potentially powerful chin of the Princess of Wales.

After her marriage to Prince Charles, Diana steadily lost weight, her healthy cheeks grew lean, and as so often happens when a young person eats sparingly, smile lines, or crow's feet as they are less flatteringly called, appeared. The unhappy news for those who acquire these lines before their thirtieth birthday is that they will age prematurely. Diana's lines

were already present in her twenties, and are today less easily 'removed' in an official portrait (even if it is the work of Lord Snowdon) than the puffiness or ageing bags under the eyes which are visible in the informal profile taken by Glenn Harvey almost seven years earlier than the Snowdon portrait.

The Princess of Wales has a large, wide right eye (seen on the left of the official portrait) disclosing a reticence to commit herself to another, but when she does, hers is a passionate, thrilling relationship. Furthermore, anyone with one eye markedly bigger than the other usually suffers from poor concentration, but has especially good powers of recall for gossip and small-talk. This last observation is especially pertinent if a person has one large eye and another which is elliptical.

Diana's left eye (on the right in the portrait) is elliptical, and above it the upper eyelid is angled acutely down towards the outer corner of the eye. This eye shape is associated with charm and jealousy, and a craving for affection and attention that most friends, spouses, or lovers will be unable to satisfy.

Look carefully at *her* right eye to see the deeply curved *lower* lid which permits a fine sliver of the white area of the eye to show. The meaning of this distinctive aspect of her right eye is that its owner suffers from severe inner disharmony. Most of us have eyebrow hairs which grow sideways or push upwards, with possibly a few pointing down towards the eyes. Diana has many growing downwards, which bespeak dissension and being at odds with family, friends, and even life itself.

Diana has attractively smiling eyes but the fine, slender, slightly curved eyelashes tell the world that if provoked she has a fiery temper peppered by vehement expressions resulting from injured dignity.

The Princess of Wales has sometimes spoken about the generous proportions of her nose, but this is a perfect nose for accumulating wealth. According to the experts of Siang Mien, the fascinating Chinese way of reading faces, a money-making nose resembles a money-saving box: wide at the top to let the money in (a wide nose bridge), and well concealed nostril apertures (that is, not visible when the nose is viewed full-frontal, as in the Snowdon portrait) so that the money will not fall out of the bottom of the savings-box.

Diana has pretty ears, distinguished by a relatively narrow notch (the scoop, or dip, at the top of the ear lobe), demonstrating that she values wealth and her privacy, and will not give her time, attention, or possessions to those she considers unworthy of her generosity, concern, or presence.

GÉRARD DEPARDIEU

This is a strikingly fascinating face that reveals an incredible amount of information about its owner, the French actor-wine-grower, Gérard Depardieu. The three outstanding features are the unusual upper lip, the big, bulbous nose tip, and the strong, square chin.

The V-dip at the top of his upper lip descends almost to the bottom edge of the lip. This V-dip lip indicates a sex drive which can best be described by a battery of powerful adjectives: forceful, vigorous, full-blooded, lusty and earthy. Tellingly, Depardieu has described his chosen career of acting for the cinema as 'like a long night of lovemaking'.

The 'diagnosis' of someone with a very big, bulbous nose tip is given in Chapter 10 as 'likely to commit an act of violence'. As Depardieu has himself admitted in front of the television cameras: 'If I hadn't become an actor I would have been a killer.' In his youth he got into regular trouble with the police, and the broken nose was acquired while sparring with an American serviceman.

A nose that is big, high, and large in every way such as Depardieu's belongs to an extrovert, bossy individual whose presence fully qualifies for the over-used description of someone 'larger than life'. This interpretation is given extra strength by his ear lobes, both of which lie at right angles to the sides of his face. A right-angled lobe typifies an individual with a compulsive influence on those who come into his presence.

There is no denying that Gérard Depardieu is a compellingly charismatic man. For the attentive face watcher, the face provides many clues to this, in particular his eyes, hair and mouth.

The smile veers from a mischievously disarming version to a sly grin accentuated by a kink, or an off-centre smirk, in *his* right corner of the mouth as shown in the photograph of the actor wearing a tie and striped shirt. At other times, he adopts a scowl or unrelenting grumpy pout, which will be rapidly replaced by a gummy grin, or an infectious whooping laugh, or a breathily uttered 'Pouf' accompanied by a dismissive shrug of his bulky shoulders. All this adds up to a swiftly changing variety of moods and unpredictable swings of emotions.

The director of the film *1492*, the $45 million epic in which Depardieu plays Columbus, the 'discoverer' of America, summed up the actor's personality: 'He's a monster. Mad . . . a force of nature', adding that if he (the director) were a woman, he would have made love with Depardieu. That Depardieu has a strong physical appeal to men and women is supported by the opinion of the screen star, Isabelle Adjani, who described him as being 'both masculine and feminine – a hermaphrodite'.

The mischievous, teasing side to Depardieu's nature can be seen in his eyes. The gaze, when he is amused or involved with someone or something, is sparkling, representing the cheeky *voyou*, or hooligan, which is the word he often uses to describe himself. On other occasions the gaze in his rather deep-set eyes is prying and challenging, the look of someone who is self-aware but at the same time confident in the knowledge that he has the measure of most comers.

Those relatively deep-set eyes also signify a certain sentimentality, while their triangular shape (discernible if you examine the shape of the folds of the upper eyelids) gives us to understand that he is a born leader. If ever he chooses to follow a political career he promises to be a genuinely inspiring leader.

Anyone with a forehead which slopes, or with eyebrows pressing as closely to the eyes as Depardieu's do, is bound to be impatient and impetuous. But in the photograph of him wearing a bow tie you will see that his eyebrows curve some distance away from his eyes; he has been caught by the camera in the middle of an eyebrow flash – a split-second raising of the eyebrows – a gesture he would make if he were greeting someone who, in this case, is off-camera.

The photo in which he looks straight at the lens shows clearly that *his* right eyebrow is straight (a mark of an achiever), whereas *his* left eyebrow is slightly arched, signalling creativity. Only rarely will you find a person with two identical or symmetrical eyes or eyebrows, and Depardieu is not one of them.

Gérard Depardieu's upper teeth slope in very slightly and there are little hollows, or indents in the corners of his mouth; together these facial characteristics tell us that he is resourceful, astute, skilful on the whole in achieving his desires and ambitions, but that he rarely allows himself to rely on others. He is fiercely independent.

Depardieu's broad, square chin is a sign of energy and enormous vitality. Add to this his strong neck and you have a clear indication that he is a naturally macho man.

Finally, his hair flops persistently over his forehead and when it is long, into his eyes, except when he throws back his head. To the face watcher this is yet more evidence of the cheeky, unruly charm of this charismatic 'hooligan'.

MONA LISA

There is endless speculation as to who Mona Lisa was and what her character might have been. It has even been suggested that the lady with the enigmatic smile could be a self-portrait of Leonardo da Vinci as a transvestite. Her smile is the most famous in the world. Some see it as having a sinister aspect, described by Sigmund Freud as expressing the contrast between 'the most devoted tenderness and a sensuality that is ruthlessly demanding'.

It is a slightly crooked smile because it is stronger on *her* left (on the right of the painting). In fact, the left corner twitches up and outwards, clearly seen in the specially commissioned profile by Rod Waters for this book. The smile suggests that she told lies and traded insults whenever it best suited her or when she lost her temper, which probably occurred frequently.

The hint of a smile playing around those much-admired lips and the distinct glint in her eyes attest to her fun-loving ways and a bawdy sense of humour. But the fact that these lips are 'bloodless' warns the face watcher of her callousness.

If you examine her lips in the portrait, which hangs in the Louvre in Paris, you will notice a small mole on her top lip. A mole anywhere on the lips or immediately above the corners of the mouth signals indigestion and flatulence. Whatever embarrassment this might have caused it does not detract from the appeal of her pretty, elongated rosebud mouth, a shape which normally testifies a romantic, dreamy lover.

Note how the upper lip narrowly overhangs the lower lip; this demonstrates her powerful sex urges, but it also cautions prospective admirers against her perfidious ways. She would certainly have been unfaithful, a characteristic additionally evident by the shape of her top lip: look at the line where her lips meet and you will see a small dip or 'V' at the base of the upper lip.

Mona Lisa holds her head and face straight and as erect as a pillar, her steady and unflinching gaze affirming her dominant personality and worldly ways. She was probably a woman of high status, a gifted abstract thinker, and would therefore in modern times be considered eminently employable.

It would appear from the angle of her jaw that it 'dropped' straight and deep below the ears. No face reading can be complete without a thorough study of the ears, which in her case are hidden, but Mona Lisa's jaw suggests that she would have been very successful in a sales career, or in publicity, public relations or in the hotel or travel industry. Moreover, a deep, smoothly rounded jaw such as hers exhibits firmness and optimism, but the beginnings of flab developing below the chin together with those plump cheeks, disclose her fondness for pasta, rich Tuscan food, and the local, full-blooded Chianti wines. Yes, she was definitely greedy.

That she was a spendthrift is evident from her nostrils, for nostrils which are visible when the face is viewed full-on, indicate their owner has a scant understanding of money, and so she should not have been given control of the family (or company's) budget. The nostrils, moreover, are narrow and the sides of her nose are flat, both features pointing to a rather untidy woman, who probably dropped her clothes, shoes, hairnets (in the portrait she wears one that flattens the top of her head) all over the parquet floor in the bedroom of a townhouse or palace near to Leonardo's hometown of Vinci, between Pisa and Florence, in Tuscany.

Because the hairnet sweeps the hair off her forehead, we can see how smoothly rounded and curved her hairline grows. This type of perfectly rounded hairline spells out a clear message: Mona Lisa was fickle, an unreliable 'friend'. Her forehead is longer and wider than the part of the face

known as the low zone, which consists of the area between the nose tip and the jawline. This facial trait tells us that she had an IQ above average, that she was a fast learner, but, being impractical and not wanting to spoil her elegant hands, she would not have been able to mend a broken vase or set a mousetrap.

A nose that is straight, long, thin and with a high bridge in addition to Mona Lisa's peculiar type of nostrils generally belongs to a witty and engaging conversationalist, but one who is impatient with those unable to keep up with the wide range of topics discussed.

A final word about her eyes: very few of us have identically-shaped eyes, but she is an exception. The eyes are narrow and elliptical, signalling jealousy, and if she suspected that another woman was after her lover (or husband), she would punish the enemy by any means, foul or fair. Mona Lisa was most definitely a sneak, but one who needed at least nine hours' sleep each night, judging by the puffy eyelids which are clearly shown in the Leonardo portrait and faithfully reproduced in the Rod Waters profile of the famous smiling Mona.

LUCIANO PAVAROTTI

With a calendar of singing engagements booked all over the world for years ahead, it is a good thing that Luciano Pavarotti's straight nose ridge shows he is a good organiser with a tidy mind.

The left side of his face is the unflatteringly named bucket shape, which tells the world that its owner is strong willed, allowing few to get the better of him in any matter which he deems important. However, Pavarotti's right side is longer, narrower, and the chin is more pointed. He told me that he wears a beard to 'hide weaknesses around the chin', but by peering through the hairs I could detect a small, raised, almost three-dimensional fleshy area in the middle of his chin, which would suggest an attractively vital sex drive, a positive feature reinforced by his relatively wide philtrum, which is the channel between the base of the nose and the upper lip.

The left side of a face reveals the more private side of an individual; the hairs at the beginning of his left eyebrow rise vertically, suggesting the importance he places on self-reliance and a reluctance to depend on others. His right eyebrow is quite steeply arched, indicating a quizzical though kind attitude to others and their troubles.

Pavarotti's eyes are quite different from each other. The left is elliptical, a sign of amiability, though this eye shape sometimes signals possessiveness and sexual jealousy. This 'diagnosis' would be more certain if he had two almost identical eyes, but his right eye shows three white areas (on either side of the iris and, more unusually, below the iris), which denotes sensitivity, a penchant for self-examination and a search for the purpose of life in a troubled world.

His gaze is clear, steady, direct and friendly, all of which add up to charisma, one who is well aware of his appeal, but is interested in the welfare of others, and their failings. The narrower left eye reveals his need for periods of solitude, though he would rarely feel lonely. In fact, anyone with elliptical eyes, one of which is narrower than the other, is likely to thrive on being alone, and can therefore be difficult as a long-term partner.

The man is loaded with common sense, as evidenced by the fact that his eyebrows slant towards the centre of the ear. That wide, rounded forehead tells the world that he is also intelligent. And that slight M-hairline denotes artistry and enjoyment of being in the limelight. Moreover, creativity and artistic gifts are evident in most individuals with Pavarotti's type of nose tip: round, fleshy and quite plump.

The ear is distinguished by its moderate-sized notch (the dip or scoop at the top of the lobe). Pavarotti's signals the extent of his generosity,

left-left

right-right

Pavarotti's two left sides
joined together.

His two right sides
joined together.

which can be great to those whom he considers merit his love and liking for them, but is reduced if he suspects that someone is trying to take advantage of him.

The ear lobes are quite fleshy with a moderately thick pad of flesh at the top, revealing that the man would have been capable of earning well even if he had not been gifted with a superhuman voice.

Note, however, that the ears are thin for a man of his build, showing a lack of sustained physical strength at times of stress. Meaty rather than flabby cheeks go with a need for a lot of sleep, and this facial observation is enhanced by his revealing to me that while he is on tour he makes sure to get about twelve hours' rest the night before a performance, that lunch is followed by twenty minutes' sleep 'to digest peacefully', and that he takes a twenty-minute nap before going on stage.

My three final observations of this warm and friendly man concern width: the widest part of his ear is across the middle, which signifies that he is a fine communicator, and to judge by the worldwide love of his superlative tenor voice, there can be no argument there.

Next, his very wide and prominent mole: a mole in the middle of the cheek belongs to a person who is more attracted by intellectual and cultural matters than material benefits. This might surprise his detractors, but their faces will probably bear the traces of jealousy.

The last observation is that his upper and lower lips are of equal width, revealing to the face watcher that Luciano Pavarotti gives, and needs, affection in equal amounts.

MARILYN MONROE

Beautiful, sexy, and vulnerable: these are the three factors most closely associated with the woman born Norma Jean or Norma Jeane (her original identity is so subsumed in Marilyn Monroe's public image that there is even disagreement on how her original name should be spelt). The face watcher can immediately see the three components in this fabulous face.

The smiling Marilyn is the public face, but the Marilyn shown in the full-face portrait is the real Marilyn.

Let us begin with the glamorous smiling image first. It seems to leap out of the page with the same magnetic intensity that her face did from the movie screens to billions of cinema-goers. But this face is, for the greater part, a mask.

If you look into the eyes of the *smiling* Marilyn you will see *her* left eye 'closed' or lowered in the customary bedroom-beckoning position that

the actress adopted automatically whenever cameras or human eyes were focused on her. Her enormous charisma is at once evident not only from her compulsive gaze, but note also the witty and innovative lowering of *her* right eye and you will see that she has added a wink to her bedroom-beckoning look. No other actress or Hollywood 'sex symbol' had the wit or imagination to think of doing that.

The dazzling smile is a cover up, part of her pose for public viewing, for she knew the effect and hold she had on men and women everywhere who never got tired of looking at her. She often admitted to wanting to be a 'real' actress, one who was 'perfect on camera', and so acting became a way of life. She once avowed to being a fake. That mole on her left cheek is

indeed a fake. It is inked in. In the more serious Marilyn in this full-face portrait there is no mole anywhere. From a face reading point of view the position she chose for her fake mole has no significance beyond her decision to create a beauty spot in a position not normally associated with a natural beauty spot; the natural place is either on the highest point of a cheekbone, or just above the upper lip near the corner of the mouth. Hers is a comic spot, and provides us with further evidence of her creativity, humour, and sense of fun.

Marilyn Monroe worked hard at ideas, admitting that love and work were good together, but one without the other 'is not so good'. The true, hard-working Marilyn can be detected from the serious portrait.

The forehead is wide and smooth, broadening across the hairline. Such a forehead signals imagination, in particular with words (written or spoken) and an interest in knowing about the causes and laws of all things. This might surprise you, but this face reveals a thinking-process superior to that which Marilyn's public face of glamour and sexuality suggests.

This 'diagnosis' is enhanced by the unusual combination of a wide forehead at the hairline, a hint of a V-point in the centre of the hairline, and a narrow jaw. This mixture depicts a suspicious nature and over-eagerness to please and to be seen to fit in with individuals from all spheres of activity. She wanted to 'belong'.

This face vibrates good health and wholesomeness. Note, however, how *her* right eyebrow (clearly shown in the full-face photograph) is more steeply arched than the left one; this indicates unpredictability and changing moods, especially when you see that these are her natural eyebrows, and that the flatter curve of the eyebrows in the glamorous, smiling Marilyn portrait are painted in.

The painted-in eyebrow shape evokes the female ideal of beauty, but look how *her* right eyebrow (the natural one in the full-face portrait) rises steeply at the beginning. This is a sign of the type of individual who is gullible and easily duped – by rogues, of course.

The following face reading of the real Marilyn is taken from the full-face portrait: her bedroom eyes are tender, endearing and beckoning. Very often the pupils of her eyes are dilated (big), a condition normally associated with someone who is excited or sexually roused. Somehow, her dilated pupils here, in a face that seems to be in repose, are poignant and forewarn the face watcher of her tragic life.

The partly-open mouth (her mouth is rarely closed) suggests a child-like quality, although the lavishly applied lipstick has been worked in hard to give the mouth a plump, shiny and sensuous appeal. Look closely under the lipstick at her real lips and you will see that the top lip is moderately slim while the lower is noticeably thicker. This type of mouth suggests her need for love was greater than her ability to love.

The two top central incisors are a little too big to match the rest of her teeth, telling the world that Marilyn was stubborn. The inner circle (anti-helix) of her ear is higher and more developed than the ear's rim (or helix), a further sign of her determination and stubbornness. But in the end, her determination must have been overcome by more powerful forces, and we will probably never know what happened, or why she died suddenly, in 1962.

The last word goes to her chin. Marilyn Monroe's chin is the epitome of female beauty: gently rounded and smooth, moving expressively whenever she flashed her winning smile.

PRESIDENT BILL CLINTON

The President of the United States of America is a face watcher's delight, for this is a face distinguished by some unusual traits giving a rare insight into the character of the most powerful man in the world.

That Bill Clinton is well-balanced, intelligent and adaptable to the high office to which he was elected in 1992 is demonstrated by the equal lengths of the three zones of his face: forehead, eyebrows to nosetip, and nosetip to the jawline.

The president is extremely ambitious and zealous. This is evident from the indents or slight depressions at his pulse points, which are located immediately above the temples at the places where the pulse beats on each side of the forehead.

One must look at Bill Clinton's ears for more vital clues to the character and personality of the American leader. His lobes are small and join the side of his face without a seam, or slit, and so cannot qualify as free-hanging lobes, which occur in most of us irrespective of sex or race. Ear lobes like Bill Clinton's are associated with those men and women who know their faults and weaknesses, and are prepared to rectify them, backtracking or reversing their opinions and decisions if they think there is something to gain by making, or being seen to make, wise moves or canny decisions.

Bill Clinton also has a slightly raised inner circle (anti-helix) which is higher than the outer rim, or helix, of his ears. This facial feature points to determination, pulling rank if necessary to make a point or persuade others to accept his point of view, which leaves many who are close to him flat-footed and not knowing which way the president will jump next.

Long ears such as the president's suggest a good memory, in particular for quotations, laws and regulations. His ear notch (the scoop or dip at the top of the ear lobe) is very wide, indicative of generosity and benevolent intentions (see page 16).

A skilful interpreter of faces can identify President Clinton's self-reliance and healthy distrust of courtiers' flattery by the presence of a long, flat tragus – the prominence or bump situated by the side of the face at the entrance to the earhole (see page 116).

The president's mouth is every millimetre as revealing as his ears, though it is surprisingly small for such a tall, active and energetic man. A frequent and 'typical' Clinton mouth gesture is to clench the lower lip and upper jaw tightly so that the mouth turns upwards in a convex curve that could be best described as a firm orbicular clamp. To interpret this presidential move it is necessary to note that it is also accompanied by the forward-thrust of his lower lip, giving the appearance of a shortened chin

that runs straight into his lower lip without the concave curve that occurs in most faces.

Although this mouth-play might look as if Bill Clinton is building up to a violent explosion of rage or expression of disgust, to the alert face watcher it divulges much more interesting information about the man. That temporarily protruding lower lip tells us that he is tough, demanding and combative.

The simulated orbicular clamp and the changes which follow to his lower lip and upper chin reveal an apparent insouciance, but this is not the whole picture, for the combination of mouth movements with his small mouth and downward-turning corners reveals an individual who bottles up his problems, but hopes that, by changing his mind if he thinks it necessary, and so compromising himself in the eyes of others, he might still stun everyone by getting it right in the end.

A broad, round chin such as the president's hints at good humour, and there is sufficient muscle and fleshy padding there to qualify, in the face

reader's view, as someone empowered with a vital and healthy sex drive. Unlike many individuals in high office, President Clinton's chin and jaw are not 'punctuated' in the centre by a conceit cleft (slit or dimple), which assures the world that he is not a vain man needing ego trips to bolster his confidence.

The Clinton nose is distinguished by having a meaty, chubby blob of a nose tip. Add to this its fleshy nostril wings and you have a protrait of a man who likes people and enjoys swopping and sharing a joke. But this combination of nasal features indicates someone tough on himself, who therefore also expects loyalty and high standards of commitment from his supporters, staff, family and friends.

If a nose ridge is straight it points the way to clear-thinking and a logical mind. Bill Clinton's ridge is straight until it meets the meaty tip, suggesting a diminution in the favourable mental attributes that a completely straight nose ridge implies. Add to this a nose bridge that is as moderately high as the president's and you find a person who is determined to have his say, but will give way, vacillate, or compromise if he thinks it will pay off in the long run.

Anyone having eyebrows that are much paler than their head of hair is liable to have to grow accustomed to charges made by people they hardly know, of having no foresight and no real concern for others. They can also expect friends and members of their family to complain of 'feeling neglected'. Owners of light eyebrows cannot be blamed for wondering who likes or trusts them, and if they took time out to scan the faces of some of these individuals they would certainly read there the signs of envy and jealousy.

President Clinton has pale eyebrows, and fine hairs grow in the area of the forehead between his eyebrows. This latter feature belongs to those who know their enemies, and will not easily forget, forgive, or overlook any bad deed perpetrated to harm them personally.

Owners of pale eyebrows with easily discernible hairs growing between them are usually jealous, in particular of their reputations. They want to be admired and liked, but most will spurn flattery and find insincerity repugnant.

The American president has different shaped eyes, which is not unusual because few people have identical eyes. *His* left eye (on the right of the main photograph) is called a peacock eye, its narrowness displaying (according to oriental face watchers who give this type of eye its name) a smug, self-satisfied but nevertheless charming person. If, however, his ambitions were thwarted, his response would be to increase the pressure to whirlwind proportions on himself and his dependents in order to achieve his goals.

President Clinton's right eye is called the fox eye, which is wider and has blunter corners and more areas of white showing than in a peacock eye. As its name implies, a fox eye denotes bravery and native cunning.

Neither Clinton eye is very wide, however, and both are slightly sunken, or deep-set, a combination of eye forces that hints at sentimentality. That Bill Clinton is kind is evidenced by the way he maintains eye contact with both familiar faces and the faces of total strangers he meets in the course of his work. He scans their faces with interest and at that moment they feel, however transiently, that they are the most important people on earth.

Perhaps this 'diagnosis' of President Clinton contains some contradictions about the man. Each of us behaves at times in unpredictable ways. The face simply reveals some of the contradictions of being human, which are shared even by the most powerful man on Earth.

PHOTOGRAPH **C**REDITS

NDEX

workaholic, 73
Worried, worrier, 44, 73
Wrinkles. *See* Lines
Writer, writing, 47, 48, 51, 53

Yemen, 183

Yiddish, 23

Zambia, 140, 184
Zebrowitz, Dr Leslie,
    59
Zimbabwe, 184